SPIRITUAL CLASSICS

Series Editor: JOHN GRIFFITHS

This series introduces the general reader to works from the various Christian traditions of spirituality which are of enduring value and interest but not generally accessible. It will include some well-known works which will gain a new lease of life from a fresh translation or adaptation, but the emphasis will be on texts not available in any modern English version.

All the works chosen have more than historical interest. They can speak to men and women of today in ways that will often be unexpected, often challenging, never dull. The introduction to each text helps bring the past to life by setting the author (where known) and the work in their cultural, social and historical context, and relating them to streams of thought and belief that, often unconsciously, still influence our beliefs and behaviour today.

The translations and adaptations are responsibly made from the best manuscripts and existing editions, with the prime concern being to present spiritual treasures from past ages in good, direct modern English. Period charm may on occasions be a consideration, but is never allowed to override contemporary effectiveness. The author's message is given precedence without destroying the meaning of the text.

Stripped of difficult and alienating linguistic quirks – of their own time and of other versions, most of them made in the eighteenth or nineteenth centuries – these works show a continuity of vision that makes them contemporary. In this form, they are not of yesterday, but of their time and ours.

Uniform with this volume

A Letter of Private Direction   *A 14th-century English mystic*

A Mirror for Simple Souls   *A French mystic of the thirteenth century*

A Letter from Jesus Christ   *John of Landsberg*

*The Cell of
Self-knowledge*

THE CELL OF SELF-KNOWLEDGE

Early English Mystical Treatises

By
Margery Kempe and Others

CROSSROAD · NEW YORK

1981
The Crossroad Publishing Company
575 Lexington Avenue, New York, NY 10022

Library of Congress Catalog Card Number; 81–65450

ISBN: 0–8245–0082–2

Designed and produced by Process Workshop Ltd, London
Photoset by Keyspools Ltd, Warrington
Printed in Great Britain by Billing & Sons Ltd

Contents

A Note on the Illustrations

The Frontispiece is taken from British Museum MS Faustina, B. VI. The device on p. 26, the pointing hand of God on p. 36, the figure on p. 76 and the Holy Spirit on p. 112 are from a woodcut by Michael Wolgemut showing angels praising God on the first day of creation, from the *Nuremberg Chronicles* (Latin edition, 1493). Jesus praying in the Garden of Gethsemene on p. 60 is taken from *Libro de la Oración y Meditación* by Fray Luis de Granada, printed by Sebastian Cormellas (Barcelona, 1512). The 'authors' pointing out the dwellings of good and bad spirits on pp. 48 and 96 are from *Augustinus, de civitate Dei*, printed by Johannes Amerbach (Basle, 1489). The circle symbolising contemplation on p. 122 is from the verso of the angels praising God.

The editor thanks the Librarian of Heythrop College, London, for supplying sources for Jesus praying and the two 'authors'.

Introduction

What we think of as introspection, a new awareness of self and of the importance of the individual, developed in twelfth-century Europe and expanded thereafter. It may be traced in a new 'romanticism' and personal reference in the secular lyric, and in such religious tendencies as the Gregorian reform. In this movement towards a greater self-consciousness, intellectual, moral and social analysis was accompanied by a new spiritual psychology which, by the end of the fifteenth century, had produced highly individual records of spiritual discernment and experience, not only in Latin but in the major western European vernaculars.

From the twelfth to the fifteenth centuries, the notion of vassalage still permeated not only social but ecclesiastical relationships and inevitably coloured ideas of the relations between the individual and God. Yet a new stress on contemplation by specific types and individuals, by those who had withdrawn from the world into a small community or some form of hermitage, helped to bring about a radical change in many people's understanding of the human connection with the divine. The old idea of an ascent by stages to divine love was reworked with new emphases ranging from basic examinations of conscience (as auricular confession was extended to the laity) to fine distinctions between the impulses of body or world, and the promptings of the Spirit. The humility of the lover in the refined code of courtly love, though often opposed to religious morality, had its counterpart in the self-knowledge of the contemplative.

As the Empire decayed and pastoral care was often withheld, from c. 1250 to 1350, the German mystics, writing largely in the vernacular, explored the inward kingdoms of the soul. They developed concepts of self-knowledge and self-abandonment so that Christ might be born again in the human soul. As the ideas of courtly love had spread from the Languedoc in southern France to be reinforced by analogous development elsewhere, so Rhineland mysticism, even when persecuted, spread and coalesced with other national expressions of the individualistic tendency, such as the *devotio moderna* or 'new devotion' in the Low Countries. It touched into life older, richly subversive currents of Christian spirituality, prompting a spirit best summed up by Johannes Tauler in his sermon at the consecration of Cologne Cathedral in 1357: 'Churches do not make anyone holy; it is people who make churches holy'. The flame of God burned in a citadel in the depths of the human heart and the heart had no intermediary in its relations with God.

The surviving mystical writings of late medieval England, produced by solitaries, wandering hermits, or anchorites in cells attached to churches, who directed or were directed by others to ever purer self-perception, revealed the same trend, though in a more pragmatic, often strongly anti-speculative and affective form.

'We stand in the cell of self-knowledge. We know that we do not exist of ourselves but by the goodness of God in us. We acknowledge that we receive our being and the grace that is higher than our being from him'. Thus St Catherine of Siena on the knowledge of self which enables the mystic to reach the higher levels of the contemplative life. It was the title selected by the editor of the second edition of the present collection of Middle English treatises, first published by Henry Pepwell in London in 1521, not long after the close of the particular age of English devotion which they represent. It expresses admirably their central concern.

This collection is essentially Pepwell's manual. It omits only *A Very Devout Treatise, named Benjamin ... or The Way to True Contemplation*, by Richard of St Victor, in the version of the author of *The Cloud of Unknowing*. This appears in another volume in the series: *A Letter of Private Direction*. The author was already well represented in Pepwell's selection, and so we have included two self-contained pieces from Richard Rolle's *The Amending of Life*, on the love of God and contemplation, which fit the central theme.

The first piece in the collection is an English presentation of the teachings of St Catherine of Siena (probably 1347–80). It stands for a major interest among certain English contemplatives. On her deathbed St Catherine is said to have charged the Augustinian, William Flete, a Cambridge graduate, with the continuation of her work in Siena itself (another major disciple, Giovanni Tantucci, was also a Cambridge man).

The personality and teachings of St Catherine proved so attractive in medieval Europe that a number of legends grew up around them; these are often as delightful and in spirit as truthful as they are factually untrustworthy. The *Legenda Maiora* of her confessor, Raymond of Capua, is the main source for details of her life. The *Dialogo* and some of her letters and prayers are the chief sources for her spiritual teachings. The *Lyf of saint Katherin of Senis the blessid virgin* was translated by a Dominican, edited by Caxton and printed by Wynkyn de Worde in London (c. 1493); it is a version of Raymond's *Legenda*. The same printer published in 1519 an English version of the *Dialogue*, by Brother Dane James. The *Divers Doctrines devout and fruitful* newly translated here are taken from the *Lyf*.

Catherine became a Dominican tertiary when very young, but chose not to enter the full religious life: 'My cell is not to be made of stone or wood; instead it will be the cell of self-knowledge'. Letters to saints and sinners, ecstasies, visions and penance, instruction of followers, advocacy of a new crusade, assured utterance in the names of Christ and of the

Holy Spirit – Catherine as revealed in her *Dialogue* and the writings of her disciples is one of the most extraordinary figures of medieval mysticism. She was not a theologian but spoke by the voice and the Master within to whom she surrendered herself entire, and whose own gift of himself to her made her speak to others with such fierce conviction. A major topic in her discourse is her knowledge of self, of her own nothingness which leads to profound humility and leaves room for clear vision of what is essential: love of God, of others and of oneself. The way to the divine union, the road from basic creaturely fear and self-concern to pure love, is revealed in love of one's neighbour and in love of the Church.

Catherine, however, was not concerned with the soul's ascent to God 'in itself', but with the means by which personal sanctity could help the Church in the world. Her concept of holiness is eminently christological: self-knowledge and awareness of one's own nothingness before God lead to a love which is united with Christ's own saving love, and to a great mission: bringing to others the news of this redemptive love. Her message is non-speculative and non-analytical; it is based on a sure experience and conviction of Jesus' saving power, but it is then directed outwards to all who need that same power. Catherine might therefore be said to stand for that movement in mystical thought which stressed mission to the world, not flight from it, and which found its best expression outside the strict community life and fine analysis of degrees of approach to God. The extent of her concern can be judged not only from the quality of her spiritual address, but from such extraordinary facts as that she, a woman in an age when they least of all might think of self-assertion, demanded that the Pope should return to Rome from Avignon and threatened him with dreadful punishments if he did not do so. Perhaps Catherine's attraction for such Englishmen as the famous mercenary, Sir John Hawkwood (one of her correspondents), was in no small way due to such evidence of independence of spirit, to her strong opinions, ardour of spirit, and that 'intuitive' understanding of truth which has always appealed to the English.

Given the general condition of women and their submission to male domination of the outward life of the Church and of society, Margery Kempe of Lynn is another outstanding figure of her age. But she did not, like Catherine, win international fame; she did not order the Pope in Rome to be about his duty or dream of a crusade to end all crusades; and she did not, as far as is known, correspond with any disciples. When Pepwell published her treatise as given here, it was the only source for her life. It had appeared twenty years earlier, printed by Wynkyn de Worde, as '... a shorte treatyse of contemplacyon taught by our Lorde Jhesus cryste, or taken out of the boke of Margerie kempe of Lynn'. This quarto of seven pages was the only trace

16

of her 'boke' (supposedly that of a devout anchoress of King's Lynn in Norfolk) until in 1934 Colonel Butler-Bowdon asked the Victoria & Albert Museum to repair the binding of a fifteenth-century manuscript once in the possession of the Mount Grace Carthusians and thenceforward handed down in his Catholic family. It turned out to be the lost *Book of Margery Kempe*.

She was born in the 1370s and married in her early twenties. She was probably illiterate, though the daughter of a man several times mayor of Lynn. Even though her husband was a freeman, if one of modest means, she decided that she had married beneath her station. She went into business on her own account – first brewing then milling – but was unsuccessful. She decided to repent of worldly desires and wished to lead a wholly chaste life. For two years, 'She thought that she loved God more than he loved her'. Three years of penance, prayer but also fierce temptation ended with another conversion. She and her husband made a vow of chastity, and she found that Christ (as he often did) agreed with her decision to make a pilgrimage to Jerusalem. After an arduous and sometimes ecstatic voyage, which included a visit to Rome, she returned to Lynn, where she and her husband lived apart – though she cared for him in his old age. She was charged with heresy, a Franciscan turned the people of the town against her (her shouting and demonstrations had already angered them), and she just escaped burning. She never spared the clergy (she did not hesitate to tell the Archbishop of York and the Mayor of Leicester that they were hypocrites), and apparently emerged triumphant from several interrogations and arguments. In spite of all the accusations of fraudulence and of importation of dangerous continental enthusiasms (the pragmatic English feared that she might have become a troublesome Flagellant while on pilgrimage), she knew the articles of faith and her Bible well, and imbibed much important religious literature from others, notably from a young priest who read to her from St Bridget of Sweden, Bonaventure, Walter Hilton and others.

All Margery's meditations are based on sound knowledge of Scripture which she amplifies with often racy colloquial dialogue revelatory of character – of her own and others – which is sometimes reminiscent of Chaucer and Dunbar. Though at times we sympathize with her long-suffering husband and the contemporaries who found her unbearably egotistical, we soon recognize her folk psychology and knowledge of self in neurosis and anger, which enabled her to reveal her traits dangerous and valuable and, through anecdote, dramatic encounter and self-reference, to enliven the necessarily derivative structures of her meditations. Her imagery brings the biblical examples into her own age: Jesus' body was 'fuller of wounds than ever was dove-cote of holes'; 'She often wanted her head to be cut off with an axe on a block for the love of our Lord Jesus Christ', and Jesus tells her that if she can only be patient that is worth more to him than having her head chopped off three times a day every day for seven years. She can reduce the contemplative life to plain terms: Christ tells her to 'speak to me in your mind, and I shall give you exalted meditation and true contemplation'. He tells her that a hair-shirt, bread-and-water fasting and a thousand Our Fathers a day are no use compared with letting him speak in her soul. Her retorts have that basic directness of folk understanding that we find in works as far apart in time as Langland's poem *Piers Plowman* and Pasolini's film *The Gospel according to St Matthew*. When she was publicly weeping in Norwich out of compassion for our Lady's suffering during the Passion, a priest rebuked Margery for being as naive as she was noisy; she answered: 'Sir, his death is as fresh to me as if he had died today, and it seems to me that it should be so to you and to all Christian people'.

Margery Kempe tells us in her book that she knew the work of Walter Hilton. He was a canon regular of St Augustine at St Peter's Priory, Thurgarton, near Southwell, where he died c. 1395. Perhaps he was a hermit before that; perhaps he died a Carthusian. He was certainly one of the leading English mystics and wrote his *Ladder of Perfection* for an anchoress. As befits an Augustinian, the main theme of the book is the human struggle to find God, and the workings of

God's love in the soul as God seeks to bring it ever closer to him.

The Song of Angels is a prose treatise traditionally ascribed, together with *The Letters to a Devout Man in Temporal Estate*, to Hilton. Like the works of the author of *The Cloud of Unknowing*, its profound mysticism is indebted to the Pseudo-Dionysius, for its theme is the perfect union of the soul with God in perfect love, which demands a clarification of the rational mind, a purging of physical imagery, that can never be managed perfectly in this world. What Hilton is writing is a kind of mystical psychology, showing the loving soul how to pick out false feelings from those that one might ascribe to love burning in the affection and to knowledge shining in the rational mind.

Elsewhere Hilton defines the three degrees of contemplation as: 1. knowledge of God and of spiritual things, reached through the exercise of reason, learning from others, and studying the Bible; 2. 'love burning with devotion', feelings of love and spiritual ardour that don't rely on intellectual knowledge; 3. 'love burning with contemplation', a more inward form of contemplation, depending not – like the second degree – on the natural senses, but on spiritual faculties.

Among an exceptional group of mystical writers of the period, Hilton himself was most unusual in his concern for those who had to live the contemplative life 'in the world', in an active condition. In spite of the highly-refined analysis in his known works of the degrees of contemplation and the qualities of self-awareness that it requires, his writing has a 'practical' reference that relates it to Catherine's interest in the active Church, or to Margery Kempe's rumbustious expression of the still small voice in the soul. As he comments when translating the *Meditations on the Life of Christ* of James of Milan: 'Anyone is really blessed who serves our Lord with Martha in the active life, yet at the same time rests at our Lord's feet sitting with Mary. That is exactly what the angels do perfectly, for they serve us in this world and yet they can see God's face in heaven. Exactly the same thing is done by someone who works to serve a 'holy' or a sick person or does any other kind of work for the love of God, and yet sees only "our Lord Jesus Christ" in the one whom he serves. "He feeds his brother and God feeds him".'

The author of *The Cloud of Unknowing*, to whom the next three treatises in the present collection are ascribed, also acknowledged that the active life was 'fully good and fully holy', and a way to perfect love. His letter on discretion was written to help the person under his direction to distinguish between good and evil inclinations of the soul. His letter on prayer and his letter on discerning spirits are also highly-nuanced essays by a master of spiritual psychology, and a very practical man. Again they display the pragmatic

English approach to the soul's ascent to God. Though he speaks of the highest things, the author's imagery is often taken from everyday life and enlivened by touches of humour; sometimes he rises to the super-real, as when he remarks that after confession a soul is like a clean sheet of paper that cries out to be written on. We can imagine one of those gorgeously perfect pieces of new pressed parchment so virginal that we might, like the French poet Mallarmé, scruple to write even at the margin's edge. Yet there are the two parties, God and his angels, and the fiend and his angel, both eager and able to write superlatively well, straining for the permission of the sole arbiter, the free-choosing soul.

The name of the author of these three connected treatises is unknown. He was probably a Midlands priest and even an ex-religious, a spiritual director writing between 1370 and 1400. He wrote with a specific individual (and similar types) in mind. In the light of his own experience, and in the vernacular, he followed the influential example of the *Mystical Theology* of the Pseudo-Dionsyus who was thought to be Denis the Areopagite who followed St Paul (Acts 17; 33), and who was commissioned by Paul to hand down a special wisdom suitable ultimately only for a select few. Here again the emphasis put upon the lessons of the Pseudo-Dionysius have a practical bent: a Christian's self-awareness and personal responsibility in searching for the right way to reach and receive God's love, was very important. The contemplative was not a passive object of mysterious forces but capable of knowing the self and, under sympathetic guidance and with grace was able to reconstruct the self, temper the ego and realize the ultimate direction of self.

Richard Rolle (perhaps born at Thornton Dale in 1300 and died c. 1349) was probably a Yorkshire man who studied at Oxford and entered the eremitic life when still quite young. He is also said to have studied theology at the Sorbonne in Paris. His major works are the *Incendium amoris* or *Fire of Love* (translated into English by Richard Mysin in 1434–5), *The Form of Perfect Living*, the autobiographical *Melos amoris* and the *Emendati vitae*, or *Amending of Life*.

Of all our authors, Rolle is perhaps the farthest removed from abstract ideas of contemplation. The goal of his contemplation is love, which is the essence of oneness with God. Since the three-personed God is ultimately inaccessible to human cognition (on which contemplation, be it ever so refined, necessarily depends), love of God is the 'concrete' aspect of contemplation on which we must concentrate if we are to come close to its mysterious goal. This sweet ravishing fire of love may be perceived with or without the physical senses. Heat is Rolle's central image, which he develops into a highly calorific scheme, approaching the condition of poetry and far distant from the cold formalism of the scholastic theology which he rejected. He attacked moral corruption in the Church as fiercely as he did pedantry. He showed deep compassion for the poor and a contempt for the oppressor which refute pictures of him sometimes put about as one who rejected earthly charity in favour of divine love. Even though writing much of the time for the anchoress Margaret Kirby, and perhaps a few others, his works reflect the transitions of his own spiritual experience, not only the quiet reception of the fire and music of love, but his many wanderings, clothed in rags like Bunyan's Pilgrim, from cell to cell, bearing his message of love to the suffering. It is not too fanciful to hear the note of the Russian *starets* in his work. He is certainly the most passionate and lyrical of the early English mystics. He was accused of many faults: of neglecting charitable works for selfish contemplation; of neglecting contemplation for charitable works; and of eating with the rich. Familiar charges.

Self-knowledge was one of Rolle's chief recommendations. As he says in an earlier section of the *Amending of Life*: ' "Blessed are the poor in spirit, for theirs is the kingdom of God". And what is this poverty of spirit but the meekness of mind in which a man can see his own weakness clearly?' That is the keynote of all these treatises.

* * *

The texts on which the present edition is based are

essentially those of Pepwell's edition, after collation by Edmund Gardner with Harleian MSS 674 and 2373, Caxton's *Lyf* of St Catherine, Wynkyn de Worde's pamphlet edition of Margery Kempe's treatise and the Cambridge MS Dd v. 55 of the *Song of Angels*. Books 11 and 12 of Rolle's *Amending of Life* have been retranslated from the 1434 version by the Carmelite, Richard Misyn.

John Griffiths

PROFITABLE TEACHINGS FROM THE LIFE OF THE BRIDE OF CHRIST CATHERINE OF SIENA

beginning with what our Lord taught her and continuing with what she taught her followers

The first thing our Lord taught her was this:

'Daughter, do you not know who you are and who I am? If you know these two things, you are blessed and will continue to be so. You are she that is not, and I am he who is. As long as you keep an awareness of these two facts in your heart, your enemy the devil will never deceive you, and you will be able to slip easily out of all his traps. You will never give way to temptation to do anything against my commandments and teachings, and you will have no difficulty in winning my grace, truth and love.'

*   *   *

The second thing he taught her was this:

'As long as you think of me, I shall think of you.'

When she told people about this saying of the Lord's, she used to say:

'A soul that is truly united to God is not conscious of itself; it neither sees, nor loves itself, nor anyone else, but keeps its thoughts on God alone, not on any creature.'

She would explain thcsc words more fully by saying:

'A soul in this state sees that in itself it is nothing, that all its virtue and all its strength belongs to God, its maker, alone. So it abandons itself and all other creatures completely and takes refuge in its creator, our Lord Jesus Christ, to such an extent that it casts all its spiritual and physical actions wholly on to him, in whom it sees that it will find every blessing and the fulness of goodness. This means that it has no desire to look for anything outside this intimate knowledge of him, for any reason whatsoever.

Being united in love in this way – a love which increases day by day – the soul becomes as it were changed into our Lord, so that it can neither think, nor understand, nor love, nor be conscious of anything but God or what belongs to God. It sees itself and all other creatures only in God; it loves itself and all other creatures only in God; it is only conscious of itself and of all other creatures in God, and is conscious only of the presence of its creator. And so,' she used to say, 'there is nothing that should concern us other than to think how to please him to whom we have entrusted everything that we do both in body and soul.'

*   *   *

The third thing our Lord taught her, about how to acquire virtue and strength of mind, was this:

'My daughter, if you want to acquire virtue and strength of mind, you must follow me. It would have been possible for me, thanks to the divine virtue that is in me, to have vanquished the evil one in any number of ways. I chose, however, to do it only by accepting death on a Cross, so as to give you an example in my humanity. So if you want to overcome your spiritual enemies, you must learn from this example to take up your Cross as I did. If you keep my sufferings on the

Cross in mind, you will find this a great comfort in times of temptation. The sufferings of the Cross might well be called comfort in temptation, since the more sufferings you bear for love of me, the more like me you become. And if you can share in my sufferings, then you can share in my joys.

So, daughter, learn to suffer the harsh things of life with patience, and not only its delights, for the sake of my love. Do not be afraid: you will be strong enough to bear everything patiently.'

* * *

The first thing St Catherine taught was this:

'A soul that is truly united to God will hate its own sensuality as much as it loves God. Loving God naturally leads to hating sin, since this is an offence against God. So, seeing that the cause and first stirrings of sin lie in the bodily senses, and that this is where it operates most freely, the soul is moved most powerfully and with all the holy strength God gives it to attack its own sensuality. It will not be able to destroy its sensuality root and branch: this is not possible as long as a soul is attached to a body in this life; there will always be a section of root left in the ground of the soul, consisting of small minor sins. Because it is unable to destroy the root of sin in its sensuality completely, the soul becomes extremely annoyed with its sensuality, and this develops into a holy hatred of this sensuality, and a great contempt for

31

it, which keep the soul well away from its spiritual enemies. There is nothing like this holy hatred for keeping the soul strong and secure against temptation.

'This is what St Paul meant when he said, "For it is when I am weak that I am strong" (2 Cor. 12: 10), meaning that when his sensuality has been weakened through hatred of sin, then his soul is stronger and more powerful. This hatred brings forth virtue; this weakness produces strength; this annoyance leads to delight. This holy hatred makes people humble, and makes them think humble thoughts about themselves. It makes them patient in times of trouble, and moderate in using the good things of this world when they have them. It sets them on the honest course of virtue, and causes them to be loved by God and by their fellows.

Without this holy hatred, we are led to inordinate self-love, and this is the polluted source of all sin, and the root cause of all evil desires. And so,' she would say, 'your first concern must be to put aside any such inordinate self-love, to root it out of your heart, and to plant a holy hatred of sin in its place. This is the sure way to perfection and the only way to turn aside from sin.'

*   *   *

This is what she used to say to the devils who assaulted her:

'I put my trust in my Lord Jesus Christ, and not in myself.'

* * *

This is a rule she gave for how to behave when we are tempted:

'When you feel temptation welling up in you,' she advised, 'never start arguing or querying. That is exactly what the devil most wants you to do – to start questioning him – because he is so confident in the subtlety of his evil powers being able to get the better of you through crafty arguments. So you should never ask the devil questions, nor answer the questions he asks you. Turn to devout prayer instead, and put your trust in the Lord not to let you give way to the devil's clever demands. Prayer and a firm faith will enable you to overcome any temptation the devil may put in your path, however subtle.'

* * *

This is a sensible discourse this holy woman gave us on how to avoid the devil's temptations:

'It can happen,' she said, 'that sometimes some fault or some new, cunning temptation of the devil will make a soul that loves our Lord lose its fervour and become turgid and dull-witted, or even down-right frigid. This can be so discouraging for some foolish people that they think they have lost the spiritual comfort they were used to having. So they abandon the spiritual exercises they used to practise –

33

prayer, meditation, spiritual reading, the eucharist and penance – and thereby leave themselves more readily open to succumb to the wiles of the devil. There is nothing the devil wants more than that Christ's warriors should abandon the weapons with which they used to be able to defeat their enemies. A prudent warrior for Jesus should never do this; instead, whenever he sees, or feels, that he is becoming dull, slow or cold in his devotions, he should not give up his spiritual exercises, but rather redouble them.'

*   *   *

This is another of this holy woman's meditations, something she used to say to herself for the edification of other people:

'You miserable, wretched creature, do you deserve any sort of comfort in this life? You poor sinner, what do you think you can do by yourself? Don't you think it's enough for you to be freed from everlasting damnation through the great mercy of our Lord? You should consider this reward enough, even though your soul should suffer every sort of torment and desolation every day of your life. So why are you distressed and cast down by these sufferings, when God's grace has undoubtedly allowed you to escape so many of the sufferings endured by Christ, and will surely bring you eternal reward if you bear these present sufferings patiently? Did you choose to serve our Lord only for the sake of the consolations he could bring you in this life? No, for the sake of the reward he would bring you in the happiness of heaven. So pull yourself together, don't give up your spiritual exercises but redouble your efforts in them.'

*   *   *

This is how she answered the devil after he had long threatened her with intolerable suffering, and so won a final victory over him:

'I have chosen sufferings to be my refreshment, so it is not hard for me to bear them. I can rather rejoice in them for love of my Saviour, for as long as he may be pleased I should bear them.'

*   *   *

This is something else she said, about to make the best use of God's grace:

'Anyone who can use God's grace in this way will soon achieve victory in everything he or she does: what you need to do,' she said, 'is think to yourself, whenever anything new happens to you, whether it brings you good fortune or bad: "There is something I can gain from this". If you can do this consistently, you will soon be rich in virtue.'

*   *   *

And now, finally, here are some noteworthy things she taught her followers the last time she addressed them before her death, which they noted down. The first of them is this:

'Whoever you are, from whatever walk of life, if you want to serve God truly and come to full knowledge of him, you must empty your heart of all love belonging to the senses, not only love for certain special people, but love for anyone at all, and make your soul reach up to our Lord and Creator alone, with all its strength and with all your heart's desire. A heart can only be given completely to God if it is freed from all other loves, so that it has become whole and open, with no hint of deceit left in it.' She said that her main concern from her youth till that moment had been to reach this state of perfection.

She went on to say that this state of perfection, in which the heart is completely given over to God, cannot be reached except through a life-long practice of fervent prayer. This prayer must be rooted in humility, proceeding not from any confidence in oneself and one's virtues, but from the knowledge that of oneself one is nothing. This, she said, had been her constant endeavour, to give herself up to the practice of prayer, so that it became second nature to her, since she saw that all the virtues are increased and greatly strengthened through prayer, whereas without it, they decline and weaken.

So she encouraged her followers to persevere in prayer, and told them about two sorts of prayer: vocal and mental. Vocal prayers, she told them, should be said at the hours of the day and night laid down by the Church in the divine office. Mental prayer, however, must become a constant habit of the soul, so that it is practised at all times.

She said, too, that her lively faith had enabled her to see that whatever happened to her, or to anyone else, came from God, not through any ill-will he might bear his creatures, but from his overwhelming love. This same faith, she went on, also bred in her a loving willingness to obey the commands of her religious superiors as though they were God's commandments, accepting them as coming from God, either for her own good or to ensure an increase of virtue in her soul.

Another thing she said was that if people wished to be truly pure in soul, they must take care to refrain from passing any sort of judgment on their neigh-bours, and from idle gossip about what their neighbours might have done. Instead, they should see nothing but God's will in everyone. So we should not judge people in any way, not seeking to condemn them or think ill of them even if they openly commit sin. What we should do is feel compassion for them, and pray for them, not feel superior to them and blame them.

Finally, she said she put all her hope and trust in divine providence, since she knew from experience that divine providence was a wonderful thing, and that it would never disappoint those who placed their trust in it.

Thanks be to God

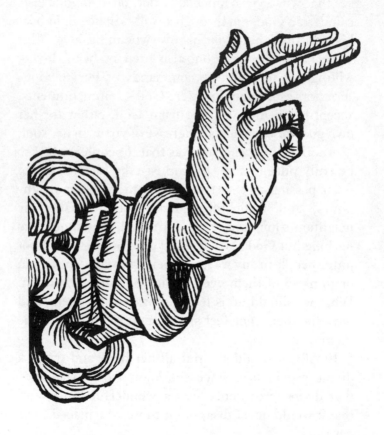

A SHORT TREATISE ON CONTEMPLATION

as taught by OUR LORD to MARGERY KEMPE

Anchorite of King's Lynn

She often wished her head could be struck off with an axe on the block to show how much she loved our Lord. When she thought this, Jesus would say to her inwardly:

'I thank you, my daughter, for being willing to die for love of me. You will be rewarded in heaven for all the times you have thought this, and it will be as if you were suffering the death you wish for, but no one is killed in heaven.

'And I tell you that if it were possible that I should suffer again as I did on earth, then I should be willing to go through all those sufferings again just for the sake of your soul, rather than lose you for all eternity.

'There is no better way of pleasing God, my daughter, than thinking about his love all the time.'

She asked our Lord what the best way of loving him was, and he told her: 'Be conscious of your own wickedness, and think about my goodness.'

He went on:

'If you wore a cilyx or hair shirt, fasted on bread and water and said a thousand "Our Fathers" every day, you would not be as pleasing to me as you are when you keep silence and allow me to speak in your soul.

'Telling your beads all the time is all right for those who can do no better, but it is not the perfect way, though it is a help towards perfection. The trouble is, my daughter, that those who are always fasting and doing penance are convinced that this is the best way of life. So are those who go in for endless devotions, and so are those who are continually giving alms. All these would like their way of life to be regarded as the best. But I have told you many times that meditation, sorrow for your sins and contemplation of the highest mysteries make up the best way of life. Your reward for one year of thinking about me in your mind will be greater in heaven than it would be for a hundred years of vocal prayer. But you don't believe me, and go on telling your beads.

'If you knew, my daughter, how precious your love is to me, you would never do anything except love me with all your heart.

'If you want to be raised up to heaven and be with me, never stop thinking about me, even at meals. Remember that I am in your heart and know every thought you think, good or evil.

'I have suffered greatly for your love, my daughter, so you have good reason to love me greatly; I have paid a high price for it.'

She answered him, saying:

'Dear Lord, let me never, I beg you, know any other happiness on this earth except that of sorrowing and weeping for your love. I sometimes think that even if I went to hell, hell could not bother me provided I could sorrow and weep for your love there as I do here. I would think it rather a kind of heaven, because your love drives all fear of our enemy the devil out of me. If you wanted me there, I would rather be there and

42

pleasing to you there, than be here and displeasing to you. So, dear Lord, if this is your will, let it come about.'

* * *

She used to wonder at the fact of our Lord becoming man and suffering such torments on her behalf, when she was so ungrateful to him. Then in great distress she would ask him how best to please him, and the answer that came in her soul was again: 'Be conscious of your own wickedness, and think about my goodness.' This led her to pray over and over again, in these words:

'Out of your great goodness, Lord, have mercy on my great wickedness, which can never be as great as your goodness, even if I wanted it to be, since you are so good that you could not possibly be any better. So I amazed that anyone should ever leave you for all eternity.'

* * *

When she looked at a crucifix, or saw a wounded person or animal, or if she saw someone beating a child, or whipping a horse or some other animal, it was like seeing our Lord being beaten or whipped just like the child or animal.

The more her love and devotion to our Lord increased, the greater grew her sorrow and contrition, her meekness and humility, her fear of the Lord and her consciousness of her own weakness. So if she saw a

43

person or animal being punished or beaten, she would rather be in their place, since she thought her ingratitude to God made her deserve punishment more than they did.

* * *

Another thing our Lord said to her was:

'Nothing you can do or say, my daughter, can be more pleasing to God than believing that he loves you. If I were able to weep with you, then I should, so great is the compassion I feel for you.'

Then our Lord Jesus Christ in his mercy drew her into his love and gave her insight into his passion. This made her unable to bear the sight of a leper, or anyone with open wounds, without weeping, since she thought she saw our Lord suffering in them. And so she did, with her soul's eye, so that the sight of a sick person filled her heart with love of our Lord, and if she met a leper, she wanted to run to him and kiss him for love of our Lord – something she would never have dreamed of doing when she was young and rich, when she couldn't stand the sight of them.

* * *

On another occasion our Lord said to her:

'I know you wanted there to be many priests in the town of King's Lynn, so that they could keep up the divine office day and night in service, worship and praise of me, as a thanksgiving for all the goodness I have shown you in your life. Well, I promise you that you will have your reward in heaven for all the good things you wanted in your life and all the good will you have shown me, just as if you had been able to turn all your good wishes into good deeds.

'Yes, my daughter, you will be rewarded in heaven for all the good deeds you have done mentally, just as if you had done them physically.

'Another thing you will be rewarded for is the charity you have shown to those who give way to the temptations of the flesh: I know you weep and pray for them constantly, asking me to rescue them from their sin and show them the forgiveness I showed to Mary Magdalen, so that they might find the grace to love me as much as she did. I know you would like to see every fallen woman given as much money as she needs to live on, so that she would be able to love and serve me freely. I am delighted with this charity you show in your prayers for them.

'I thank you too for the charity you show when you pray that all Jews, Muslims and pagans will be converted to the Chrstian faith, so that my name can be glorified in them. Also for the charity you feel for all living people, and for all those still to live, till the end of the world. You have told me you would like to be cut into small chunks of meat for the cooking pot if this would save them all from damnation.

'So for all these good and charitable feelings of

45

yours you will be rewarded in heaven, never doubt it in the least.'

She replied: 'My good Lord, for the sake of your love I would be tied naked to a hurdle, where everyone could come and stare at me and throw muck and trash all over me, and be dragged from town to town for the rest of my life, if this pleased you and did not endanger anyone else's soul. But your will be done, and not mine.'

*　　*　　*

Again he spoke to her and said:

'Whenever you say: "Blessed be all the holy places in Jerusalem, where Christ underwent his bitter trial and passion", you will receive the same indulgence as if you had gone there in person. This is the indulgence you were granted earlier, which was confirmed on the feast of St Nicholas: full remission of all your sins. It is granted not only to you, but to all those who have faith in the fact that God loves you – and to all those still to be born who will have the same faith – and who give thanks to God for you. Provided they turn away from their sins, make a firm purpose of amendment not to sin again, are sorry for those sins they have committed and do proper penance for them, they will all be granted the same pardon as was granted to you at Racheness, which is the same as all the pardons to be obtained in Jerusalem.'

*　　*　　*

If a day went by without suffering some grief for the sake of our Lord, she was not as cheerful or happy as she was on the days when she did suffer for him.

Jesus said to her: 'Patience is a higher thing than performing miracles. It gives me more pleasure, my daughter, to see you suffering contempt, scorn, shame and every manner of ills than if your head could be cut off three times a day for seven years.'

'Lord,' she answered, 'in your great sufferings have pity on my little sufferings.'

When she was greatly distressed, our Lord said to her: 'I must comfort you now, my daughter, because you are now on the right road to heaven. This is the road that I and all my disciples followed. Now you are better able to understand what trials and tribulations I went through for love of you, and you can feel greater sympathy for me when you think about my passion.'

'My dearest Lord,' she answered, 'shouldn't you be giving these graces to priests and religious?'

'No, my daughter,' he said, ' I shouldn't, because they don't love the things that I do: contempt, scorn, shame and the mockery of other people. So they cannot have this grace, because anyone who fears to be put to shame in this world cannot come to perfect love of God.'

LETTER TO A FRIEND
on hearing
THE SONG OF ANGELS
by WALTER HILTON

My dear friend in Christ,

From what you have told me and what I have heard from a mutual friend, I understand that you would like to have more knowledge and understanding of what is meant by 'the song of angels', or divine harmony. I believe you want to know what it is, how it can be felt in a person's soul, and how one can be sure that it is real and not imagination. Also how one can tell whether it comes from a good spirit and is not put into a person's soul by the wiles of an evil spirit.

It would be nice to be able to tell you everything you want to know about these things, but quite honestly I can't be sure what the real truth of the matter is. Let me try, though, to tell you briefly what I think.

You must know that the aim and fulfilment of perfection consist of union between God and a person's soul through perfect charity. This union is brought about when the powers of the soul are brought by grace to that state of elevation that we call the 'first stage'. This is when the mind is firmly fixed, without deviating or wandering, on God and the things of the spirit, when the reason has been purged of all concerns of the world and the flesh, when the mind no longer dwells on human ideas and imaginings, but is so enlightened by grace that it can contemplate God and spiritual things; when the will and the affections have been cleansed and stripped of all human and carnal love, and are inflamed with a burning love of the Holy Spirit.

No one, you understand, can remain in this state of union all the time or to the full extent in this life, because a mortal body cannot support it: for that we have to wait for the bliss of heaven. But the degree to which a soul can approach this unity in this life indicates the stage of perfection it has reached. The more it comes, through grace, to resemble the image and likeness of its Creator in this way, the greater joy and happiness it will possess in heaven.

The Lord our God is eternal and unchanging, his mighty power cannot fail, he is the height of wisdom and light, pure truth without error or distortion, absolute goodness and love, total peace and delight. So the more a soul is joined and united to our Lord, made like and turned into him, the more stable and powerful it becomes, the wiser and more enlightened it is, the greater goodness and peace it enjoys, the more loving and virtuous it will be – the more perfect, in a word. A soul that through the grace of Jesus, and through long practice of physical and spiritual exercises, has overcome and rooted out desires, passions and unreasonable impulses – the inner ones of the mind and the outer ones of the senses – and has cultivated all the virtues – humility and meekness, patience and gentleness, firmness and steadfastness, self-control, wisdom, truth, hope and love – will have become as perfect as it can in this life.

Such a soul will then receive all manner of favours

from our Lord: not only in its secret innermost nature, thanks to the union it enjoys with our Lord, which consists in knowing and loving God, burning with clear and spiritual love of him, being changed into the Godhead; it will also enjoy many other spiritual comforts and delights, and savour the sweetness of divine favour in all sorts of ways by which our Lord reveals his presence to his creatures here on earth, and through which the soul can grow and gain in charity. Sometimes, God gives such love to a soul that it is purified to the point where the whole of creation, all that can be seen or heard or felt by any of the senses, becomes a source of pleasure and joy; the senses find a new delight and inspiration in all created things. Whereas before the impulses of the senses had been tainted with original sin, so that they were hollow and evil, they are now spiritual and pure, so that they need give rise to no remorse or reproach from one's conscience.

This shows the goodness of God: where earlier a person had been punished in his or her sensuality, so that the body was made to share in the sufferings of the soul, now the soul is able to delight in the senses, and the body can share in the joy and pleasure of the soul – in a spiritual, not physical way – just as it had shared in its sufferings. This is when human beings recover, through grace, their freedom and dignity, above that of the rest of creation, when they can see the rest of creation as it really is; when, that is, they come to see and hear and feel God alone in the whole of creation. This is when the senses become spiritual through all-embracing love, when they become part of the inner being of the soul.

Then, too, our Lord gives the soul the privilege of hearing the divine harmony. There is no physical simile by which this can be described, because it belongs to the realm of the spirit and is beyond the powers of our imagination or reason. A soul can feel it and experience it, but cannot demonstrate it. I shall try, nevertheless, to tell you something about it to the best of my ability.

When a soul has been purified by God's love, enlightened in its understanding, established by his power, then its vision is opened to the things of the spirit and it can see virtues in angels and the holy souls and other heavenly things. Its purity enables it to feel the touch and hear the voice of good spirits – I mean it can do this spiritually, not physically. And once a soul has been lifted, seized up, out of its senses, and beyond consciousness of physical things, then, in transports of love and enlightenment (God willing) it can hear and feel the divine harmony, which is the sound of the heavenly choirs of angels adoring God.

Hearing this divine harmony is not the greatest privilege a soul can enjoy. Because the impurity of a human soul, bound to a body, makes it unlike the angels, it cannot hear this harmony except through the cleansing power of love; it needs to be completely purified and totally filled with love before it can hear this heavenly sound. But the greatest and most particular joy the soul can experience is the love of God in himself and for himself; seeing and communing with angels and other spiritual beings is secondary. Just as a soul can sometimes be helped to understand spiritual matters by the spirit working through human imagination, as the prophet Ezekiel saw the truth of God's hidden mysteries in his human imagination, so the spirit can help a soul caught up in the love of God to escape from all material and bodily sensations to a heavenly joy, in which it can hear the divine harmony, the angels' song of praise, provided it has attained to a high enough degree of love.

It seems to me impossible for a soul to hear the angels' song, the divine harmony, without being perfect in love; on the other hand, it is possible to be perfect in love without hearing it. For this, the soul has to be so consumed in the crucible of love that all physical elements have been burned out of it, and anything that can come between this soul and the purity of the angels has been removed and taken away from it. Then indeed can this soul 'sing a new song to the Lord'; then it can really hear the blessed harmony of heaven, the angels' chorus of praise, without pretending or being deceived.

Our Lord knows which souls have this burning love to such a degree that they can hear the divine harmony. What is essential for anyone who wants to hear it, without self-deceit or the tricks of the imagination or the wiles of the devil, is to have perfect love. This means that all false love and fear, all false joy and sorrow, have been expunged from the heart, so that it can love nothing but God, fear nothing but God, have no joy or sorrow in anything but God. Anyone who follows this road by God's grace can be sure of being on the right way.

But it is possible to be deceived by one's imagination, or by our enemy the devil, in this matter. Some people who have striven for a long time to get rid of their sins and acquire virtues through physical mortification and spiritual exercises may perhaps come to peace of mind and a clear conscience; they may then abandon their prayers, bible readings and meditations on the passion of Christ, cease to be conscious of their own wretchedness. Then, before God summons them in his own time, they take hold of their mind by the scruff of the neck, as it were, and force it to see the things of heaven. Or, before grace has made their senses truly spiritual, they can over-stress their minds through imagination to such an extent that they overtax their brains by excess effort and end up by destroying the powers and wits of body and soul. Then it will be feeble-mindedness that makes them think they hear marvellous sounds and songs. In fact, this will be pure fantasy, brought on by their deranged minds, as those who are in the grip of madness always think they can hear and see things no one else can. This is either nothing but empty-headed fantasy, or it is the work of the devil putting the hearing of such sounds into their imagination. If you introduce presumption into your imagination and actions, and so become prey to disordered fantasies, like mad people, without the ordering of the mind that grace brings, and without the support of spiritual strength, then the way is open for the devil to come into your soul and deceive you with his false enlightenment, false sounds and false comforts.

A soul then becomes the false ground in which error and heresy can flourish, along with false prophecy, presumption and false reasoning, blasphemy, slander and a load of other evils. So if you see anyone concerned with spiritual matters fall into this error and self-deception, or in a frenzy of false rapture, you can be sure that he or she is not hearing the divine harmony and never has done. Those who really hear it become so prudent that their imagination will not lead them astray, and they will be proof against the crafty workings of the devil.

Some people feel what seems like a heavenly sound, or some sort of sweet sound, in their hearts; this can sometimes be good but can sometimes be deceptive. It happens like this: they set their hearts to think only of the name of Jesus, hold their thoughts constantly on this, and in due course the name becomes a source of comfort and peace, so that they think they can 'hear' the name playing sweet music in their hearts. The

57

pleasure they derive from this is so great that all the faculties of their souls are submerged in it. If they are really hearing this sound and feeling this peace in their hearts, then this is a good thing and comes from God, and you can be sure that as long as they remain humble, they will not be deceived. This is not the divine harmony, but the soul rejoicing through the offices of the good spirit.

When a soul truly and humbly offers itself to Jesus, putting all its trust and hope in him and keeping him constantly in mind, then the Lord will, if he so desires, purify the soul's feelings, filling it with the sweetness of his presence, which will taste to the soul's feelings like honey, sing in them like sound, and be anything sweet to the soul, so that its longing for evermore is to cry out the name of Jesus. Then it will also find comfort in the psalms and hymns and anthems of the Church's worship, and enjoy singing them freely and heartily, without discord or reluctance. This is a good thing, and a gift from God, since it derives from love of Jesus, which is strengthened and refreshed by such songs of praise.

But you must be wary of a false feeling of security in such feelings; not so much when your feelings are singing to Jesus and loving him for the sweetness of his presence in your soul, but afterwards, when the moment has passed, and your heart's ardour is cooling: this is the time to beware of self-importance. You can also be led astray through being told that it is good to keep the name of Jesus, or some other divine word, in your mind; you can then make enormous efforts to do so, and teach yourself to have it always on call in your mind, but without any feeling of sweetness in your heart, of any light of knowledge in your understanding; it will be a mere abstract thought of God, or Jesus, or Mary, or any other good word. Deceit can enter in here, not that it is wrong to bear Jesus constantly in mind, but there is the danger of taking what is only a habit of mind acquired by one's own efforts for a special divine favour, and so giving it more value than it has. You must know that any abstract concept of Jesus, or of any spiritual matter, without any feeling of love or light of understanding, is a blindness and deception if you take it for more than it is worth. It is safer to be humbler in your own mind and regard it as of no value, till your feelings are fired with love, and your understanding enlightened with knowledge.

There, I have told you something about this, I think. I am sure there is more to say, and I am not sure that all I have said is correct. If you think differently, or if others are inspired by grace to contradict me, let me leave you with this thought (and leave the word to others): for me, the main thing is to rely on faith and not on feelings.

60

THE LETTER ON PRAYER

My dear spiritual friend in God,

Since you have asked me how you should control your feelings when you are praying, let me give you the best answer I can.

Let me start by saying that the best thing you can do when you start to pray, however long or short your time of prayer is to be, is to tell yourself, and mean it, that you are going to die at the end of your prayer. I am not joking when I tell you this: just think how impossible it is to tell yourself – or for anyone living to tell himself or herself – that you are certain of living longer than the time your prayer takes. When you think of this, you will see that it is quite safe to tell yourself that you are going to die, and I advise you to do so. If you do, you will find that the combination of your general sense of your own unworthiness combined with this special feeling of how short a time you have left to make a firm purpose of amendment, will concentrate your mind wonderfully on a proper fear of the Lord.

You will find this feeling taking real hold of your heart, unless (which God forbid), you manage to coax and cajole your false heart of flesh with the false security (which can only be a false promise) that you are going to live longer. It may well be that you are going to live longer. It may well be that you are going to live beyond the time of your prayer, but it is always a false comfort to promise yourself that this will be the case and to persuade your heart to rely on it. This is because only God can know the truth of the matter, and all you can do is rely blindly on his will, without having any certainty beyond this for a moment, for the time it takes to blink an eye.

So if you want to pray wisely, or 'sing psalms with all your art' (Ps. 47: 7), as the psalmist counsels you to do, make sure you work your mind into embracing this proper fear of the Lord, which, as the same psalmist tells you later on, is 'the beginning of wisdom' (Ps. 111: 10). But for all that this is a proper feeling, beware of relying on fear alone, in case you get depressed; so follow this first thought of your imminent death with another: think firmly that whether God's grace allows you to get through to the end of your prayer, dwelling on every word as you go, or whether you actually die before you get to the end, you are doing what is in you to do, and therefore God will accept it from you in full satisfaction of all the times you have wilfully strayed from the straight and narrow path from your birth till that moment. What I mean is this: provided that you have previously, to the best of your ability and following the dictates of your conscience, confessed your faults as the Church requires, then this short prayer, however little a thing it may be, will be sufficient for God to bring you to salvation if you should die in the act of saying it; and, if you live longer, it will be a great increase of merit in you.

This shows God's great goodness; to quote the

Psalms again: 'none who seek refuge in him are brought to ruin' (Ps. 34: 22). Since this process of seeking refuge has two sides to it: forsaking evil and doing good, there is no better way of getting these two aspects working in you than spiritual concentration on these two thoughts. What can get a person out of the habit of sinning better than really feeling a fear of dying? And what can more readily move a person to doing good than sure and certain hope in God's mercy and goodness, which this second thought brings about? Indeed, a spiritual clinging to this second thought, truly allied to the first, is a real basis for hope to cling to in all your efforts to do good.

If you hold fast to this hope, you will surely be able to climb the mountain of perfection: that is, advance in perfect love of God, even though you are now only in the early stages, as I shall go on to explain. Your general impression of God's mercy and goodness and your special experience of his mercy and goodness in accepting this little service of your prayer as full redress for all your earlier waywardness, must make you feel a great impulse of love for him who is so good and kind to you. The hope you cling to will show you his goodness and kindness while you pray, if you concentrate on the two things I have already mentioned. You will find spiritual evidence of the operation of hope in the reverent feelings of love for God that you have while you are praying, brought about by the proper fear of the Lord combined with loving impulses inspired by hope. Reverence is nothing other than fear and love mixed together and added to this sure and certain hope.

The operation of hope, it seems to me, will be seen in devotion, which as the learned doctor St Thomas has taught, is nothing but your willingness to do those things that belong to the service of God. People can prove this for themselves: if they serve God in this way, they will feel how ready their wills are to do so. St Bernard would seem to agree with this, when he says that everything should be done swiftly and with gladness in one's heart. Swiftly, out of fear; with gladness, out of hope and loving confidence in God's mercy. What else can I say about this? Just that I would rather be someone who can persevere in such service, even without doing any penances other than those enjoined on us by the Church, than any of those great doers of penance from the beginning of the world to this day. By this I do not mean that there is so much merit just in thinking the two thoughts, but that the loving reverence which these two thoughts do so much to bring about is worth more than all the penance in the world.

This loving reverence alone, without any other practices (such as fasting, going without sleep, wearing hair shirts and the like) is pleasing to almighty God and deserving of reward from him. Without it, it is impossible to receive any favours from him, and the degree of favour received will depend on the degree of loving reverence felt; those who feel a lot, will receive many favours; those who only feel a little, will receive fewer. These other practices, such as fasting, going without sleep, wearing hair shirts and so on, are worthy only in so far as they bring about the loving reverence; unless they have that effect, they are no use. But they are sometimes not necessary to bring about this loving reverence, which can be enough in itself and can come about without any of these other practices. I am telling you all this so that you can come to appreciate each thing for what it is, prizing the greater more highly and the lesser less highly: ignorance in these matters can often lead to much misunderstanding. It can lead people to set more store by this sort of physical exercise – fasting, lack of sleep and the like – than by spiritual practice of the virtues or this loving reverence I have been describing. So I propose to go on and say more on the subject of this loving reverence, to enable you to gain a better appreciation of it than you already have.

The way in which it works, when it has been ushered in by the two thoughts I have described – fear and hope – may be compared to a tree laden with fruit; fear is the part of the tree below ground: the roots; hope is the part above ground: the trunk and branches. The trunk represents the stability and certainty of hope; the waving branches represent the way it impels people to acts of love. Loving reverence is the fruit, and as long as the fruit remains on the tree, it is second-class merchandise, since it still has the greenness of the tree about it; once it has been picked and allowed to ripen fully, and has lost the sharpness it had while it was still on the tree, it is first-class fare. This is when this loving reference is so full of merit.

So prepare to pluck the fruit from the tree, and offer it up on its own to the King of heaven; then you will be called a child of God with good cause, since you will then be loving him for his own sake, not for the sake of the favours he can bestow on you. I mean by this that though God's innumerable favours to people in this life are good enough reason – and more – for them to love him, with all their minds, hearts and wills, yet if it were possible – which it isn't – for someone to be as powerful, deserving and intelligent as all the angels and saints in heaven put together, without having received any favours from God, or without having known God's kindness in his life, this someone could still be so smitten with the beauty of God in himself and the abundance of grace that his heart would burst: so lovely and loving, so good and so glorious is God in himself.

God's love is a marvellous and excellent thing to talk about, yet no one can really grasp the smallest part of it, or describe it except through the most far-fetched examples, which are beyond the reach of human understanding. This is what I mean by loving him purely with love for himself, not for his favours, which I have not dwelt on much (though I might well), since he in himself is so far above comparison with them. If I can try to describe what I mean by this loving reverence I have spoken of, and how perfect and deserving it is, I would say that a soul which has been granted a feeling of God's presence as he is in himself – a perfect soul enlightened in its reason by God's clear beam of eternal light, by God himself, that is – so that it sees and feels the beauty of God as he is in himself, must, for the time this experience lasts, lose all consciousness of any favours God may ever have done to it, and know no other cause to love God than God himself.

If one is talking about commonly-experienced degrees of perfection, God's great goodness and the degrees of kindness he shows us in this life are certainly grounds enough for loving him. But if we are talking about the very highest degrees of perfection (which you are aiming for and which I am trying in this letter to encourage you to reach), then the perfect lover of God would be afraid to risk marring his perfection by allowing any other reason for loving God to creep in except God himself. This is what I mean by saying that pure love of God consists in loving him for himself and not for his favours. So, to go back to my comparison with the tree and the fruit, prepare to pluck the fruit from the tree and offer it on its own to the King of heaven so that your love will be pure; while you offer him an unripe fruit still hanging on the tree, you will be like a woman who marries a man for his money and not for himself – and you can't call that pure and disinterested love! If you are as diligent in serving God as you are out of fear of dying and a feeling that you haven't enough time left to be sorry for your sins (as I suspect you are), then you are like such a woman, and your offering will have a sharp taste to it; it can still be partly pleasing to God, but it cannot please him fully, because your love for him is not yet pure and disinterested.

Your love will be pure when you no longer ask God to relieve your sufferings, nor to increase your merits, nor even to give you more enjoyment of his love in this life. If a time comes when you wish for enjoyment of his love as a means of refreshing your spiritual powers, so that they do not let you down on your way, and you then ask nothing of God but himself, taking no heed of whether you are suffering or happy, provided you can have him whom you love – then this is pure, perfect love. So be ready to pluck the fruit from the tree, to rescue your loving reverence from the fear and hope that went before, so as to be able to offer it ripe and whole to God by itself, with no thought for anything that is lower than God, or in which God plays only a part (even though it be the main part), but thinking only of God himself, in himself; then this loving reverence is as deserving as I have said it is.

All those who are practised in the science of divinity and who have advanced far along the path of God's love are convinced that whenever a person is drawn to

God without any intermediary (by which I mean without any go-between in the shape of a particular thought which brings on the impulse to love) then that person is meriting eternal life. And since a soul drawn to God in this way – offering him the fruit ripened off the tree – can be suddenly caught up to God innumerable times in the course of a short space of time, it deserves to be raised up in joy more than I can say, through God's grace, which is the chief agent in this process. So, as I have said, be ready to offer the fruit ripened off the tree. The fruit still on the tree, if offered up continually because that is all human weakness can manage, is enough to win salvation; but perfection consists in suddenly offering up the fruit ripened off the tree, without intermediary.

I am trying to show you that the tree is good in itself, even though I am advising you to pluck its fruit to make that more perfect. I put it in your garden because it is good, and I want you to pluck its fruit and keep that for your Lord. So now I should like to go on to tell you how a person's soul comes to be bound up with God and united to God in love and singleness of purpose; as St Paul says: 'Anyone who is joined to the Lord is one spirit with him' (1 Cor. 6: 17). For all that God and the soul are two beings different in kind, they can be so bound up together in grace that they become one in spirit; this is brought about by singleness of will and of purpose, and this singleness brings about the spiritual marriage between God and the soul, a bond that can never be broken (though the passion can go out of it for a while) except by grave sin.

In this state of spiritual union, the loving soul can say (or sing, if it has a mind to) the wonderful statement from the Song of Songs attributed in the Bible to Solomon: 'My Beloved is mine and I am his' (2: 16), meaning 'My Beloved loves me and I love him'. In this union God's bond is formed with what one might call the spiritual glue of grace, and yours is formed by your loving consent in joy of your spirit.

So climb the tree, and when you reach the fruit (the loving reverence I have spoken of, which will always be in you if you keep the two thoughts that bring it about continually in mind, and provided you don't flatter yourself with any lies), you will have a good idea of the way this loving reverence operates in your soul at that moment. Then be ready, as far as grace permits you, to humble yourself before the majesty of God; this will enable you to use the operation of this loving reverence on its own at other times, without needing to climb up to it by any thoughts. This is what is so deserving in itself, as I have said, and the longer it is kept away from the tree (from any thoughts, that means), and the more it can come into operation suddenly and boldly, lovingly and without inter-mediary, the sweeter it will smell and the more pleasing it will be to the King of heaven.

When you feel delight and comfort in this working of loving reverence, then God is sharing the fruit and giving you back part of the gift you gave him. And when you feel that everything is hard and going against the desires of your heart, so that you can feel no sort of delight from the outset, this means that the sourness of the fruit still hanging on the tree, or only just picked from it, is setting your teeth on edge. But it will still be beneficial to you, because you cannot reach the sweet kernel without first breaking the shell and biting through the sharp pith. But if your teeth (your spiritual powers) are weak, I advise you not to try too hard, as skill will often prevail where brute force is no use.

There is another reason why I put this tree in your garden for you to climb. However true it is that God can do whatever he wants, as far as I can see it is impossible for anyone to reach the perfection of this work (of loving reverence) without the two earlier means I have described, or another two like them. Yet the process comes to its peak suddenly, and without intermediary. So I advise you to take these two things as yours, not as possessions, because what you possess is nothing but sin, but as gifts from God, sent through me acting here as his messenger, unworthy though I am. You must know that any thought that impels you towards God, whether it is spiritually provoked in your own mind or given to you by an outside human agent, is an instrument of grace sent by God to work in your soul. And this is why I am telling you to hold on to these two thoughts above all others: just as a person

73

is made up of two natures, physical and spiritual, so two different ways of reaching perfection are needed; just as both these natures will be united when we are raised from the dead on the last day, each can be raised to perfection in this life by an appropriate means. These means are fear for physical nature and hope for the spiritual. This, it seems to me, is just as it ought to be, because exactly as there is nothing like a proper fear of dying to tear the body away from attachment to earthly things, so there is nothing like sure and certain hope of being forgiven for all one's waywardness to lift a sinner's soul up to the love of God.

This is why I have laid down these two thoughts as the means by which you should climb toward perfection. But, of course, if you find that your own spiritual promptings, or someone else, can show you two others that suit your character better than you think these do, you must feel free to follow their counsel and forget the two I have taught you. But in my view (and till I learn otherwise), I think these two should stand you in good stead, and be suited to your character, as I see it. So, if you find them good for you, give thanks to God for this in your heart, and remember me in your prayers, which I stand more in need of than you can know.

That's all for the present. May God bless you, and you have my blessing too.

Read a lot, and remember what you read. Face trials bravely, and keep away from temptation and occasions of temptation, for the sake of our Lord Jesus Christ, Amen.

A MUCH-NEEDED LETTER ON MODERATION IN SPIRITUAL IMPULSES

My dear friend in God,
God grant you the same blessings and joy that I would wish for myself.

You ask me to give you some advice on the subjects of silence or conversation, ordinary dieting or rigorous fasting, living in community or all alone. You say you are very doubtful about what you should do, since on the one hand you find yourself drawn – like most people – to the pleasures of conversation, shared meals and living with other people, while on the other you fear having to keep silence, fast rigorously and live alone, since you feel this will make you out to be holier than you are, and bring other dangers. These days there is a tendency to regard those who fast rigorously, keep silence and live alone as the holiest people, and yet they often fall into the greatest dangers.

If grace alone leads them to fast, keep silence and live alone, and their nature merely acquiesces in the action of grace, then they are indeed holy. But if this is not the case, if they are forcing their natures to fast, keep silence and live alone, then they are in great danger from all sides. Grace is the only cause that should lead people to do things beyond the common measure when these things are in themselves morally indifferent, sometimes good and sometimes bad, sometimes working with you and sometimes against you, sometimes a help and sometimes a hindrance. If you follow your impulse to be different, straining every sinew to keep silence, to fast rigorously or to live alone, you might find yourself being silent when you should be speaking to people, fasting when you should be sharing a meal with your friends, living alone when you should be in a community. On the other hand, if you always open your mouth when you feel like it, always enjoy meals in common and the joys of companionship, then perhaps you will sometimes be speaking when you should be silent, eating when you should be fasting, in company when you should be alone. This can easily lead you into error and cause confusion to your own spiritual well-being and that of others. So you ask me two things about avoiding such errors (as I see from your letters): first, what I think about you and your spiritual impulses; and second, what I would advise in your case – and in others like it.

On the first matter, whether I am writing to you or to anyone else, I would hesitate to make a judgment, for two reasons: I do not trust my own opinion enough to be able to state with certainty that it is the right one; I do not know as much about your inner state of mind, and your aptitude for the things you speak of in your letter, as I should need to if I were to advise you fully on such matters. As the Apostle Paul so rightly says: 'After all, the depths of a man can only be known by his own spirit, not by any other man' (1 Cor. 2: 11). Furthermore, even you may not yet know your own mind as well as you will later on, when God has shown it to you through a course of trials and successes. I have never yet known a sinner (as we all are) fully aware of his or her own nature and disposition until taught in God's school, where the lessons are the experience of temptation and the course a succession of failures and successes.

A ship sailing on the sea will pass sometimes through waves, floods and storms; sometimes through gentle airs, calm waters and fair weather before sighting land and reaching harbour. So with the soul on its passage through the ebb and flow of life: it will encounter trials and temptations (the waves and storms of the sea) on the one hand, and the grace and goodness of the Holy Spirit will give it comfort and peace (the gentle airs and calm waters) on the other. Like the ship, the soul will eventually reach the harbour of health in the land of stability. This harbour is self-knowledge, understanding one's inward nature, and brings a great calm, like that enjoyed by a king governing his kingdom with power, wisdom and sense, and governing himself, body and soul, in the same way. Such a one is meant by the Apostle James: 'Happy the man who stands firm when trials come. He has proved himself, and will win the prize of life, the crown that the Lord has promised to those who love him' (James 1: 12). The crown can stand for two things: one is spiritual wisdom, balance and perfect virtue, which can together be called a crown of life and the channel for grace in this life; the other is the everlasting joy which souls that have been steadfast in this life will enjoy in the happiness of heaven. In both cases, we can only win the crown if we have 'proved ourselves' in the trials and temptations of life, as the Apostle James said; or, in other words: unless sinful humanity has been put to the test through a series of temptations, sometimes winning, sometimes losing – losing through human weakness, winning by God's grace – God cannot give it spiritual wisdom to know itself and all its quirks clearly. Nor can people who have not themselves been put to the test acquire the balance needed to teach and advise others, or the perfect virtue which consists in loving God and one's neighbour. These three – wisdom, balance and perfect virtue – go together, and together can be said to make up the crown of life.

A crown contains three elements in its make-up: gold is the first, precious stones the second, and the fleur-de-lys raised above the circlet the third. Gold stands for wisdom, the precious stones for balance, and the fleur-de-lys for perfect virtue. Gold surrounds the head, and wisdom governs every side of our spiritual endeavours; precious stones gleam so that by their light we can see other people, and balance enables us to teach and counsel others; the fleur-de-lys has two branches, one going to the right and the other to the left, and through perfect virtue (which means charity) we hold out two branches of love, one on the right to our friends, another on the left to our enemies. There is even a third, reaching up to God, beyond our understanding, which is the captain of our soul.

Such is the crown of life, which is the channel for grace in this life; so be humble in your trials, and submit meekly to your temptations till you have 'proved yourself'. Once you have done this, you will be able to take either crown, or both – the one in this life and the other in the next. Those who win the one in this life may be sure of winning that in the next, but there are those who go through the trials of this life and never receive its crown. Provided they humbly go on accepting that this is the Lord's will for them, they can be sure of the other one in heaven. You may set high store by the crown to be won in this life, but be as humble as grace allows you to be about this, because by comparison with the other to be gained in heaven, it is small change in a world full of gold. I am telling you this to comfort you and make you take heart in the spiritual struggles on which you have embarked trusting in the Lord, and at the same time to show you how far you still are from complete understanding of your true nature, and so to warn you not to trust overmuch in, or follow too swiftly, the more extreme impulses of your young spirit, in case they let you down.

So I am telling you this to show you what I think of you and your impulses (as you asked me to do). I can see that you are able and willing to give rein to your impulses to indulge in rigorous practices: this can be very dangerous. By this I do not mean that your ability and willingness – or those of anyone else similarly

inclined – are wrong in themselves, however dangerous they may be. No, I certainly don't mean this, and
heaven forbid you should think I do. They are good in
themselves, and a most valuable means to achieve
perfection – even the greatest perfection to be found in
this life. Provided, of course, that those so disposed
are prepared to humble themselves to God's will night
and day, to seek good advice, to face their trials
bravely and be ready to suffer the martyrdom of their
own intelligence and will when they feel themselves
subject to sudden and excessive impulses, telling
themselves firmly that they will not be ruled by such
urges, however attractive they may seem at the time,
and however noble and holy – unless these are
encouraged by spiritual directors well versed in
dealing with extraordinary gifts. Then, if they
persevere humbly in their spiritual efforts such people
may well deserve to win the crown in this life through
the grace and experience gained in a continuous
spiritual struggle with themselves. But, just as these
impulses can be an aid to development in a soul that is
prepared to follow this path of humility, so they can be
a great source of danger in others that rely on their
own intelligence and will, seek no good advice and
blindly follow the dictates of their own hearts. So, for
the love of God, mistrust your own abilities and
impulses in these matters, if you think what I have
said applies to you. Be humble in continually striving
to pray and to seek good advice. When you feel these

extraordinary and sudden impulses, fight your own intelligence and will; don't follow them blindly until you are sure of their source, and whether they are the right thing for you.

So, since you asked for my advice on the subject of your impulses, I must say that I regard them with some suspicion, particularly if, as I suspect, they have something of aping of others about them. Apes, as you know, are supposed only to be able to imitate – if my suspicions are unfounded in this respect, forgive me. But the spiritual affection I feel for you compels me to say, on the evidence of a brother of yours and mine in the spiritual life, that I think they may be well-founded. He felt the same desire for strict silence, rigorous fasting and living entirely alone, but after long talks with me, and facing his own impulses squarely, he admitted that he was aping someone else – someone from your part of the world who, he said, is famous for silence, fasting and solitude. In his case, I am sure these are the product of grace within him, and not based on what he has seen and heard of other people – he would be aping in his turn if they were, if you will excuse the expression.

On this evidence, then, I can only say: be careful, and face up to your impulses squarely and find out truly where they come from – whether they are the product of an inner grace, or of aping someone else. God, not I, knows the truth of the matter. But if you want to avoid the dangers in these impulses, I ask you again to look them squarely in the eye and find out whether it is really the inner promptings of grace making you want to be silent or to speak, to fast or to eat, to live alone or in company, and not just the outward sensations that press on your senses, your ears and eyes: in other words, make sure you're not being an ape. As the prophet Jeremiah says, 'Death has climbed in at our windows' (Jer. 9: 20), that is, through our outer senses.

I have said enough on the first question: what I think of you and of the impulses you told me about in your letter.

To come to the second question: as to the advice I can give you (and anyone else who feels the same way), I can only call on Jesus (who is called the angel of good counsel) to be your counsellor and comforter in your trials and needs, and to help me in his wisdom by inspiring my teaching so that – simple and ignorant as it is – it will be worthy of the trust you have placed in me, rather than in others, even though I certainly do not feel holy or wise enough to teach you or anyone else.

But, since you have asked me to, I shall endeavour to say something, despite my ignorance, trusting that God will make good the defects of my natural powers and my professional learning. So: you yourself know well enough that the choice between silence and conversation, fasting and eating, living alone or in community, is not an end in itself. Some people, though not all, find the hard choice between these a helpful means to the end, provided they make it in keeping with the laws of the Church and with moderation; otherwise it can be more of a hindrance than a help. I don't think I can advise you at this moment to opt for strict silence, full fasting, complete solitude: perfection does not consist in these things alone. As a piece of general advice, I would tell you to hold all such impulses in check where there are two opposites involved: silence or conversation, fasting or eating, solitude or company, normal Christian dress or the special habits of various orders – all these, after all, are only natural considerations and things devised by men. It is only your outward nature that advises you to be silent or to speak, to fast or to eat, to live alone or with others, to wear ordinary clothes or a special habit, even if you feel that any or all of these things would be a help in increasing grace in your soul.

Beware above all – you and anyone else who feels the same way – of being so ignorant and blinded that you fall into the worst trap set by the noonday devil: to make some special vow binding you to any such unusual practices (except the normal vows of the religious life). Such vows may have a veneer of holiness about them, but they are the final contradiction of the freedom brought by Christ, which is the spiritual cloak of the greatest holiness to be found in this life or the next, as Paul says: 'Where the spirit of the Lord is, there is freedom' (2 Cor. 3: 17).

So, once you have seen that all these things can be either good or bad, my advice is to set them all aside, which is the best course if you are being truly humble, and stop worrying and trying to find out in your own mind which is the better. Put the strict way on one side and the lax way on the other, and look instead for what is hidden between them; once you have found this you will be free in spirit to pick up or leave any of the other things as you wish, without needing to feel any guilt at your choice.

What, you may ask, is this hidden something? Quite simply, *it is God*. If you ought to be silent, it is for his sake; if you ought to speak, it is for his sake; if you ought to fast, it is for his sake; if you ought to eat, it is for his sake; if you ought to be alone, it is for his sake; if you ought to be in the company of others, it is for his sake – and so on for any other course where you have a choice. Silence is not God, nor is talk; fasting is not God, nor is eating; solitude is not God, nor is company; and the same goes for any other pairs of opposites. God is hidden between them, and you cannot find him with your intelligence, but only through the love you feel for him in your heart. Your reason cannot know him, your thought cannot encompass him, your mind cannot comprehend him: he can only be loved and found through the truly loving impulse of your heart.

So choose him, and you will be silently speaking, speaking silence, eating in fasting, fasting in eating, and so forth. This loving choice of God, knowing what to set aside in order to seek him out with the steadfastness of a pure heart, being able to put both opposites aside when they present themselves as the be-all and end-all of spiritual aspiration, is the best way of finding God you can learn in this life. This applies to those who want to be contemplatives, because if you try to see God through the eyes of reason, you will see nothing; whereas if God is the object of your love and the reason for your existence, the choice made by your heart and its final desire, this will be enough for you in this life, even if you see nothing of him through the eyes of reason. Even a blind shot with the arrow of burning desire never fails to find its mark, God, as the Bible says in its great love song, where God speaks to the soul languishing for love of him, and says: 'You ravish my heart, my sister, my promised bride, you ravish my heart with a single glance from your eye' (Song of Songs 4: 9).

The soul has two eyes: reason and love. Reason can tell us how powerful, wise and good God is through the evidence of his creatures, but not in himself; once reason fails, then the exercise of love comes into play, because through love alone can we feel him and find him, and hit the mark which is God himself. This eye of love is a marvellous thing, for it is only of the loving soul that God says, 'You ravish my heart'. The eye of love, blind to so many things except the one thing it seeks, will find and hit its mark, go far more directly to the point than if it could see all sorts of other things – as reason can, and so is forced to pick and choose among them: things like silence or conversation, fasting or eating, solitude or company, and all the rest . . .

Forget reason's way of looking at things, and behave as though you did not know they existed (as means of finding God), because if you want to be a true contemplative and soon achieve your aim, they should not exist for you. So, with the Apostle Paul I beg you and others like you, 'to lead a life worthy of your vocation' (Eph. 4: 1). If your calling is to be a true contemplative, imitate Mary and set your heart on 'the one thing necessary': God himself. Make him the object of your will and your search, your love, your object, your aim and your support: not through silence or speaking, fasting or eating, wearing hair shirts or comfortable clothes. Sometimes it can be a good thing to keep silent, but it might be better to talk, whereas at other times it can be good to talk, but better to keep silent, and the same applies to all the others – fasting, eating, solitude, company and so on. One can be good and the other better at any particular time, but none can ever be the best. So let everything that is good be good, and what is better be better, knowing that they will all fail you and come to an end one day. You cling on to what is best, with Mary, your soul's mirror, who will never let you down: 'Mary has chosen the best part; it is not to be taken from her' (Lk 10: 42). This best part is Jesus, who said that Mary, the example all contemplatives should follow, had chosen the best part, which should never be taken from her. So, I beg you, follow her example: leave the good and even the better aside, and choose the best.

Leave all these things alone: silence or speech, fasting or eating, solitude or company, and the like, and don't bother about them; you don't know what they mean, and it's not worth your while trying to find out. If you find yourself having to think about them and talk about them, merely say that they are wonderful aids to perfection, since knowing how to speak, how to be silent, how to fast and how to eat, how to be alone and how to keep company, are talents so far above your humble abilities that it would be dreadfully presumptuous of you to speak of such perfect matters. We can of course do any of these things naturally when we want to, but really *knowing* how to do them is a different matter, and such knowledge can only come to us through grace.

This grace will certainly never come to us through keeping strict silence, through rigorous fasting or through living alone in the ways you mention in your letter, since these are only things learned outwardly by watching and listening to what others have done. If we are to have this grace, it has to come to us from within, from God; and it will only come in this way after long days spent in loving contemplation of God, putting everything that is lower than God out of our mind, even though some of them may strike other people as excellent means for getting to know God. Let them say what they will, but do as I advise you, and let the proof of the pudding be in the eating. Those who would rapidly reach their spiritual goal need one means, and only one: the mind of the good God himself, reached through the generous impulse of unfailing love, so that the only way to God is God himself.

If you keep intact the impulse to love that you feel in your heart, and don't allow yourself to be distracted from it in any way, then your loving feelings will be well able to tell you when to speak and when to keep silence. They will be a wise guide to you, teaching your unerringly, though in a mysterious manner, what to do at all times, when to start something and when to finish. If grace and continual practice keep these feelings working in you, they will be the first to tell you, in a small, still voice, when to converse with other people, when to eat with them or live with them, or to do any of the other normal things that the general run of Christian people do. Then if you don't do them, these feelings will act like a spur to your heart and give you no rest until you do them.

Conversely, if you happen to be talking or engaged in any other normal activity when you ought to be keeping silence, or whenever you ought to be doing the opposite of what you are doing: fasting instead of eating, living alone instead of with others, or any other practice that is a mark of special holiness, then these feelings will not let you rest till you are doing what you ought to be doing. So contemplatives learn how to speak or to be silent properly, how to eat or to fast, how to live alone or in company, and everything else of the kind, sooner from their experience of blind love of God than from any excessive practices prompted by their own intelligence and will, or from following the example of others, whatever they may be doing. If you force your nature to do something, without being moved by grace, you will suffer discomfort without deriving any benefit from it – unless, of course, you are doing it under religious obedience, in which case the benefit derives simply from the act of obeying, not from the outward forcing of nature, which is a painful process, as anyone who has tried it will know.

But if you freely and willingly embrace the love of God, you will enjoy a great peace surpassing anything else, a true spiritual peace which is an intimation of the eternal peace of heaven. So speak when you want to and stop when you want to, eat when you want to and fast when you want to, live alone when you feel inclined to and in company when you feel the need for it, letting God and grace be your guide in all things. Let those who want to fast do so, those who want to live alone do so, but hold on to God who will never let you down; whereas fasting and eating, living alone and in company can all let you down at one time or another.

So if you see people eating or fasting, living alone or

with others, think, and say out loud if you want to, that they know what they are doing, unless this is obviously not the case. But don't do what they do (just *because* they are doing it, I mean) like an ape: either you won't be able to, or it just won't suit your character. So stop following what other people's natures tell them to do, and do what your own tells you to do, if you know what that is. And until you learn what it is, follow the advice of those who do know their own natures – but don't imitate them. Such people should give advice to people like you, but no more.

I think I have answered all the points in your letter, so God's grace be with you always, in the name of Jesus. Amen.

96

A TREATISE ON DISCERNMENT OF SPIRITS,

necessary for those who wish to lead a spiritual life

Since there are different kinds of spirits, we need to be careful to distinguish between them. As the Apostle John teaches us, we cannot believe them all: 'It is not every spirit, my dear people, that you can trust' (1 Jn 4: 1). It may seem to those who have little understanding of spiritual matters that every thought that comes into a person's mind can only be put there by that person's own spirit. This is not the case: David shows in the psalms that we can listen to the voice of God: 'I am listening. What is Yahweh saying?' (Ps. 85: 8). And the prophet Zechariah speaks of 'the angel who was talking to me' (Zech. 1: 9). Another psalm tells us that the wicked spirits send people evil thoughts. Besides this, Paul shows that there is a bad spirit of the flesh, who can lead us astray and give us a false sense of importance: 'people like that are always going on about some vision they have had, inflating themselves to a false importance with their worldly outlook' (Col. 2: 18). He shows also that there is a spirit of the world, when he rejoices that he himself and his followers have received the message, 'not only as words, but as power and as the Holy Spirit' (1 Thess. 1: 5).

These two spirits, of the flesh and the world, are servants or henchmen of the wicked spirit, the foul fiend himself, the prince of hell; he is the spirit of evil itself, and he commands the spirit of the flesh and spirit of the world. We should not trust any of these spirits when they speak to us, whichever one it may be, because all of them are out to ruin us, body and soul. We can tell which of the three is speaking to us at a particular time by the tenor of what he says to us: the spirit of the flesh is always going on about ease and comfort, the spirit of the world encourages us to vanity and seeking honours, and the spirit of evil puts dark and bitter thoughts into our minds.

So whenever we think about food and drink, soft beds and comfortable clothes, sexual pleasures and anything else belonging to the realm of the flesh, and feel our hearts burning within us, as it were, with desire and longing for all these things, then we can be sure that the spirit of the flesh is suggesting them to us. And whenever our hearts are filled with thoughts of the hollow pleasures the world can give – being thought handsome or beautiful, having gifts showered on us, being socially acceptable or regarded as highly intelligent or respectable, or holding important positions or high office – all such thoughts, and others which can make people seem important, not only in the eyes of others, but in their own eyes as well, then we can be sure that it is the spirit of the world that is speaking to us. He is far more insidious an enemy than the spirit of the flesh, and it is much more important to know how to deal with him.

Sometimes these two henchmen of the devil, the spirit of evil and prince of darkness, can be firmly put down and trodden underfoot by grace and the spiritual powers of the soul. Sometimes, however, their crafty and malicious master, the ruler of hell himself, cunningly calls them back, so that he himself can pounce on our simple souls like a lion on its prey. This is what is happening whenever we are seized not with lust or the desire to be important, but with the urge to gossip and complain about other people, nurse grievances against them, feel bitter about them, hurt by them, cross and impatient with them, full of self-pity, ill-will, hatred, envy and the like. Then we react sullenly to whatever people say or do to us, instead of with the graciousness we know we should show; we go about looking to see if other people are talking about us, suspect them of laughing at us behind our backs, take anything said about us as an insult.

All these reactions and impulses, and any others that destroy our peace of mind, are to be resisted as the devil himself. They are his fiendish devices and we must beware of them if we want to save our souls. Of course the spirit of the flesh and the spirit of the world are also working as hard as they can to make us lose our souls, but they are not nearly so cunning or dangerous as the spirit of malice: this is the evil one himself, whereas they are just his creatures and cannot exist without him. However free from the desires of the flesh and the pleasures of the world you may be, if you are tainted with this spirit of malice, bitterness and suspicion, you are on the way to perdition, even though you may not be guilty of physical or worldly sins. And if you are consumed with the passions of the flesh and the pleasures of the world, but are nevertheless well-disposed towards your fellow-Christians (though this is difficult to achieve when the world and the flesh have a firm grip on you), you are less liable to be lost, however foul your physical and worldly sins.

The lustful desires of the flesh are harmful, because they distract us from the devout life; hankering after the pleasures and honours of the world is worse, because it divorces us from the real joy we should feel in contemplating the things of heaven, as shown by the good spirits of God. If you seek honours, favours and service from others in this world, you cannot deserve the spiritual honours, favours and service that come from contemplating heaven and heavenly things all your life. These are better in themselves and a higher reward than is to be had from seeking worldly honours. But the bitterness brought by the spirit of malice and evil himself is worst of all. Why? Because it cuts us off from what is best of all: love, God himself. Those whose hearts are given over to bitterness and envy can have no inkling of the peace of the blessed souls in heaven, which is the good and merciful God's own sweet self.

This is what David is referring to in the psalm where he says: 'For Yahweh has chosen Sion, desiring this to be his home, "Here I will stay for ever, this is the home I have chosen"' (Ps. 132: 13). Sion here means the vision of peace; the soul that has this vision is the one that is at peace, and this is the one in which God will come to dwell, as he himself says through the prophet Isaiah: 'I live in a high and holy place, but I am also with the humbled and contrite spirit, to give the humbled spirit new life, to revive contrite hearts' (Is. 57: 15). So, if you want to have God living in you, and to live in loving contemplation of the peace of God, which is the best and highest object of contemplation you can reach in this life, be always on your guard to put down the spirit of the flesh and the world when they come to you, as they will, at any hour of the day or night. But be most on your guard against the spirit of bitterness and malice, for he is the real spirit of evil, the foul fiend himself.

If you are to be effectively on your guard against him, you need to know his cunning ways because ignorance is no defence against his deceptions. Sometimes the crafty devil will get himself up to appear like a good spirit, so as to be able to do more damage under the guise of virtue. But by their fruits you shall know them, and if we look under the cloak of holiness he seems to be spreading in these cases, we will find the same old seeds of bitterness and malice sown on the ground beneath. For instance, he inspires some people to affect an extraordinary holiness beyond the reach of most – and beyond the reach of their own real abilities – in the shape of fasting, wearing hair shirts and other external signs of great devotion, and going about reproving others for their faults, which they have no right to do. He spurs them on to these and many other observances which look like works of devotion and charity, not because he takes pleasure in any real deeds of devotion and charity, but because he loves the dissension and slander that arise from such inappropriate shows of holiness. If there is a community of devout people in which one or two seek to stand out from the rest by such practices, foolish folk will regard all the other members of that community as less worthy than they and think less of them in comparison, though sensible people will think less of those who try to stand out in this way. But because there are more fools than sensible people, those who try to stand out will be flattered by the majority, whereas (if things were as they should be) they and all their imitators would generally be seen as the fools, as the devil's weapons used to attack loyal but simple souls under cover of holiness and the appearance of charity. The devil has been able to deceive an awful lot of people in this way.

Those who do not give in to the devil's wiles in such matters, but stick humbly to prayer and follow good advice, will not be so deceived. But if we are honest with ourselves, we must look at ourselves and not at other people, and have to admit that sometimes we are so bound up with the spirits of the flesh, the world and the devil, so endangered, ensnared and enfeebled by all three, that we present a sorry sight to ourselves. To our own great confusion, we find that we are doing the work of all these spirits for them. That is what happens when we have got into the habit of giving in to them when they come to us; eventually we become so physical in our appetites, so worldly in our desires, and so wickedly malicious toward others, and we ourselves, without needing to be prompted by any outside spirit, engender our own lecherous thoughts, worldly vanities and, worst of all, bitter and hateful thoughts about other people, backbiting and slander, suspicions and judgments on them.

Once we have got into such a state, it is difficult, I admit, to know whether our own spirit is making us do these things, or whether these other three spirits are acting on us. But in the end, what does it matter whether it is us or them, when the result is the same? What does it benefit us to identify the cause when the whole effect is evil? If the cause is the enemy without, don't give in to him, but humbly pray and seek good advice, so that you will be able to resist him with force. If it is the enemy within, reproach him bitterly and be heartily sorry that you ever fell into the devil's clutches to such an extent. Confess the habits you have got into, and your old sins, so that God's grace will enable you to win your freedom back again. Once you are free again, you will be able to tell – and see from the effects – when it is your own spirit acting in you and when it is one of these other evil spirits putting wicked thoughts into your head. Once you are able to tell one from the other, you will be in a much better position to resist their wiles, because ignorance is the cause of many errors, whereas knowledge enables you to avoid them. If you want to acquire this knowledge, this is what you should do:

If you are uncertain where your wicked thoughts come from, whether they are the product of your own mind or come from an outside enemy, take care – consulting your spiritual adviser and your conscience – to see that you have properly confessed and done penance (as enjoined by your confessor) for all the times you can remember giving in to that sort of sin. If you have not confessed them, do so, as fully as grace and your conscience enable you to. Once you have done this, you can be sure that any temptation to commit the same sins again will be the work of spirits other than your own – the three I have spoken about. You need not feel guilty about such thoughts, however vile and however thickly they crowd in on you, unless you are remiss about resisting them once they have come to you. If you resist them steadfastly, you will not only deserve remission of the time in purgatory you deserved for having commited these sins in the first place, but you will win grace in this life and merit reward in heaven.

You should feel responsible for any wicked thoughts you have that urge you on to sin once you have consented to that sin, and before you are sorry for consenting and make a firm intention of confessing it. You should confess such thoughts as your own fault.

But it is very dangerous to regard thoughts which you know have come to you from outside agencies as your own responsibility. You can then overburden your conscience by regarding things as sins when they are not, and this is a serious error and can lead you into great danger. If every wicked thought and impulse to do wrong came only from your own spirit and not from any outside agency, then we would have to regard our own spirit as the devil himself, and this is patently false and a damnable error. Even if our weakness and habit of falling into sin reduce us to such a state that we are doing the devil's own work for him by urging ourselves on to further sins without the need for any outside influence to do so for us, this does not make us devils by nature, but only in our actions. We could be called devilish, because our actions are like those of the devil, inciting ourselves to sin, which is the work of the devil, but we should not be called devils. However subject we are to sin, and however devilish in our actions, sorrow for our sins, confession and a firm purpose of amendment can still set us free again and put us back on the path of salvation – indeed, we can still become God's special friends in this life, however deserving of damnation we may have been before.

So, while it is dangerous not to account to ourselves for the sins we have committed, and not to resolve never to commit them again it is just as dangerous – and perhaps even more so – to burden our conscience with every wicked thought and impulse to sin that comes to us. If we load all these on to our conscience, we can come to have a false impression of ourselves, which can lead us to despair in our hearts. This comes about through not knowing how to distinguish one spirit from another. This knowledge comes from experience, as you can find out by examining your soul after it has been wiped clean in confession.

Just after confession, a soul is like a clean sheet of paper, which will show clearly whatever is written on it. On one side, God and his good spirits are ready to write on it; on the other, the devil and his evil spirits are waiting to do so. The soul has the freedom to choose who to give the pen to, and its choice is its consent to good or to evil. A new idea of sin, or a new urge to any sin which you have already confessed, can only be the work of one of the three spirits who are your enemies offering to write the same sin on the clean sheet of your soul once again. It can't be your own work because there is nothing written there; confession has given you a new sheet of paper and it is still clean. There is nothing in your soul but the power of free consent, somewhat inclined to evil, it is true, out of habit, but also somewhat more able to do good than evil through having been cleansed and strengthened by the sacrament of penance. There is nothing belonging to it at this time that will urge it either to good or to evil, so it follows that any inclinations it then has, whether to good or to evil, are not products of the soul itself, but only of its consenting to the good or evil, whichever it may be.

It is this consent, to good or to evil, that determines whether is deserves reward or punishment. If it consents to evil, then sin is making it do the work of the evil spirit that first suggested the sin to it; if it consents to good, then grace is making it do the work of the good spirit that first suggested the good to it. Whenever any healing thought comes into our mind – of chastity, sobriety, contempt for the world, freely-embraced poverty, patience, humility or charity – we may be sure that it is put there by God and his spirits: either those who are at work in this world, those who teach us the truth, or the angels in heaven, who inspire us to do good. Just as the habit of consenting to the three evil spirits over a long period can make us so physical in our appetites, so worldly in our desires and so malicious toward others that we are doing their work for them, so it is true that the practice of virtue over a long period can have the opposite effect. By clean living and spiritual vigilance we can overcome the spirit of the flesh; by concentrating our thoughts on heaven we can conquer the spirit of the world; by keeping peace and charity toward our fellows in our hearts we can vanquish the spirit of malice and evil. We will then be doing the work of the good spirits for them – in so far as the weakness inherent in this present life allows us to.

So you can now see that every thought that comes

The Cell of Self-Knowledge

into our minds, whether it is good or evil, is not always
the work of our own spirit. What is always the work of
our own spirit is the consent we give to that thought.
God grant us the grace to consent to the good ones,
and not to the evil ones. Amen. Thanks be to God.

THE LOVE OF GOD
by Richard Rolle

Sweet light, joyous light, you the unmade who made me, enlighten the contours and working of my inward eye with unmade clarity. Shine into my mind so that it is wholly cleansed and so exalted by your gifts that it rushes into the full happiness of love. Kindle it with your sweet fire so that I may sit in you, Jesus, and rest there full of joy, walking about as if ravished by heavenly sweetness and always beholding unseen things. Let me be glad in God alone.

Everlasting love, inflame my soul until I love God so much that nothing burns in me but his desires. Good Jesus, no one but you can help me so to feel you that I feel no one and nothing but you, and see no one and nothing but you. Shed yourself into the innermost depths of my soul. Come into my heart and fill it with your clearest sweetness. Moisten my mind with your sweet love's hot wine so that I forget all unhappiness and all ridiculous dreams. Let me be happy only in your presence in me and rejoice only in Jesus, my God. From now on, sweetest Lord, do not leave me. Stay with me wholeheartedly in all your sweetness, for my only comfort is your presence and only your absence can make me sorrowful.

Holy Spirit, you give grace wherever you wish. Come into me and ravish me until I am yours. Use your honey-sweet gifts to change the nature that you made, so that I am fulfilled in your loving joy and my soul despises and throws away everything in this world. Burn my longing so that my heart glows for ever on your altar. Sweet and true joy, come to me, I pray you. Come, sweet and most desired love. Come to me my love; come to me my comfort; come!

Use your sweet heat to urge longing for you from my soul. Kindle the whole of my heart with your love. With your light enlighten my inward being. Feed me with the honey-song of your love. May my soul find gladness in this and similar meditations and get to the very pith of love. Love truly suffers and assails the lover, not so that a loving soul should stay wrapped up in itself, but so that the soul is more where it loves than where the body is that lives and feels that love.

There are three degrees of Christ's love into which, one after the other, anyone is called who is chosen to love. The first is 'unable to overcome'. The second is 'unable to be parted'. The third is 'singular', or 'oned'.

Love is truly unable to be overcome when it cannot be overcome by any other desire. It cannot be overcome when the lover first throws of all hindrances and all temptations and destroys all physical desires, and then patiently suffers all unhappiness for Christ's sake, and cannot be overcome by any flattery or any inclination. To a lover all labour is light. The best way to overcome difficulties is to love.

Love truly cannot be parted when the mind is fired with great love, and draws close to Christ with all thoughts concentrated on him. Indeed, it can't allow him out of mind for even a second, but, as if imprisoned in heart, it sighs to him and cries out to be clasped to him by his love and to throw off mortal bonds, begging him to do nothing but lead it to what it desires. The lover worships and loves the name 'Jesus' so much that it is the constant preoccupation of the mind. And so, when the heart of Christ is in the heart of God's lover, and the world is despised so much that no other desire of love can overcome it, it is called 'high'. But when he or she holds fast to Christ, undeparted from Christ, always thinking of Christ, never forgetting Christ for any reason whatsoever, it is called 'everlasting' and 'undeparted'.

But what can happen to this love which is 'high' and 'everlasting'?

Well, there is the third degree, which is called 'singular'. It is one thing to be 'high', and another to be 'oned' to Christ. It is one thing to have Christ always present in one, and another to have no other companion but Christ. We may have a great crowd of companions and still reserve the first place for Christ. If you really look for some other comfort and get something from someone or something other than your God, and if you happen to love whatever it is, then your love is not 'singular'. You can see then how very great an achievement it is if you move on from the stage of being 'high' to that of being alone or 'oned'. Love ascends to this 'singular' degree when it shuts out all comforts but the comfort it finds in Jesus, and when nothing but Jesus will satisfy it.

In this third degree the soul is intent on loving Christ alone. It yearns for Christ alone and desires no one but Christ. It lives only in his desire, sighs only to him, burns only in him, and rests only in his warmth. It finds nothing else sweet and nothing else savorous. It becomes sweet only in Jesus, in whose mind all is music and song and feasting with wine. It doesn't matter what the self thinks up for itself and happens on, it will soon be cast down if it does not serve Jesus' desire and follow his will.

Whatever the self does seems pointless and intolerable unless it pushes and leads desire towards Christ.

When the soul loves Christ it believes it has all it can ever want to have. Without Christ all things become vexing and noisome. But whoever truly loves Jesus endlessly and steadfastly lives in his body, and does not become weary in heart but loves perseveringly and suffers everything gladly. The more that anyone lives like this in Christ, the more love is kindled, and the more it becomes like Jesus himself. The more the soul is ravished to the point of joy the less it is occupied by outward things, and the less it is filled with the cares and burdens of this life. Thus a soul that at the start couldn't stand even the least pain is held back by no anguish whatsoever, for it finds its joy in God always and ever.

Soul, stop loving this world. Melt in the love of Christ. Put everything else aside and discover how sweet it is to speak of him, to read of him, to write of him, to think of him, to pray to him and praise him always. God, my soul is devoted to you and wishes to see you. It cries out to you from a long way off. It burns in you. It longs in your love and in love of you. Love that never fails, you have overcome me. Everlasting sweetness, everlasting beauty, you have wounded my heart. I am so overcome and wounded by you that I fall. I am so full of joy and I can scarcely go on living. I almost die. This perishable flesh cannot stand such great sweetness, such vast majesty. All my heart is truly bound up in the love of Jesus; it becomes the white heat of love, to be swallowed into another form. Therefore, good Jesus, have mercy on this wretched creature. Show yourself to my longing self. Heal me in my sickness. Anyone who does not love you loses everything. Anyone who does not follow you is mad. So always be my joy, my love and my desire, so that I may see you in Sion, God of gods.

Charity is truly the noblest of the virtues. It is the best and sweetest of things that Jesus should be loved by the lover and that Christ should be everlastingly joined in the chosen soul. Such love remakes the image of the Trinity in us; it makes human creatures most like him who made them.

The gift of love is of more value than all other gifts, for it rivals even the high degree of angels. The more truly that someone in this life shares in love, the greater and higher in heaven he or she shall be. Joy of everlasting love, you are unique, for you turn all our longings and desires towards the heavens above all worlds, fixing them there with bonds of virtue. Without charity no one can really do anything worthwhile, whatever else he or she may have.

Anyone who is truly possessed by the spirit of charity is raised up into a joy above this world, and enters boldly the bed-chamber of the everlasting King. Do not be ashamed to take no one but Christ, for it is Christ whom you have sought and loved. Christ is yours. Hold fast to him, so that he who is the only one you wish to obey holds fast to you. Charity, you are sweet and consoling. You make whole what was broken, you free captives, you raise us up to the condition of angels. Sitting and resting you raise us up and, when raised up, we are made sweet by you.

Love in this degree or state is chaste and holy. It is concerned altogether with what is loved. There is nothing outward-looking which can please it. It lives in the soul, sweet-smelling and wholesome, marvellous and beyond belief.

It thinks of you constantly, joy whom it loves. To you it ascends in desire. It falls in love with you, goes to you to beg for favours, overcomes by kissing, and melts in the fire of love.

Christ's lover pays heed to no rank and desires no status in this life, so that he or she can be fervent and joyous in Christ's love and think more and more lovingly of him. God is truly infinite in greatness and better than ever we may think. His sweetnesses are uncounted; no created thing may ever really conceive him as he is; none of us can ever really comprehend him as if he is in himself everlastingly. But when the mind begins to burn in desire for its Maker, it is able to receive uncreated light; it is so inspired and filled with gifts of the Holy Spirit, that – as far as this is possible for human beings – it is raised up to enjoy the sweetness of everlasting life. And, while the soul is filled with the sweetness of the Godhead and the heat of its Maker's light, and is offered and accepted in sacrifice to the everlasting King, it is as if quite consumed by fire.

Happy love, you are strong, ravishing, burning and unsatisfied. I want my soul whole and entire to be in your service and to think of nothing but you. Christ is the source of your love and we love him for himself alone. Whatever is to be loved is for Christ to whom we bring everything that we love.

Perfect love is truly present when the mind's whole intention and the innermost workings of the heart are lifted up into the love of God.

Love undivided and unique, your love is so great that you would never wish any sinner to be lost. It is not your will that the wicked should suffer. An untold sorrow should be more tolerable than a deadly sin. Therefore love God for himself and for no other reason. For how could God be all in each thing if there were any physical love of human beings in one of us?

The Cell of Self-Knowledge

Clear charity enter me, take me into yourself, and present me thus before my Maker. You are a savour well tasted, a sweetness well smelled, a pleasant odour, a cleansing fire and an everlasting comfort. You enable us to contemplate; you open the gate of heaven for us. You close the mouths of our accusers, reveal goodness and hide a multitude of sins. We love you and preach you while we overcome the world by your means. We rejoice in you and ascend by means of your heavenly ladder.

Turn to me in your sweetness. I commend myself and those close to me to you for ever.

CONTEMPLATION
by Richard Rolle

The contemplative life is divided into three parts: reading, prayer and meditation.

God speaks to us in reading. We speak to God in prayer. When we meditate, angels come down to teach us so that we do not go wrong. They ascend in prayer and offer our own prayers to God, rejoicing when all goes well for us, acting as messengers between us and God. Prayer is a humble desire of the mind turned towards God which pleases him when it reaches him. Meditation on God and on godly things comes after reading, like the use of incense.

Reading depends on reason and inquiry into truth; it is like a good clear light shed on us. Prayer depends on praise and song, and contemplation is classed with prayer. Meditation relies on God's inspiration and understanding, his wisdom and aspiration.

If you ask what contemplation is, I find it very hard to define. There are those who say that the contemplative life is nothing but the knowledge of the future and of mysterious things, or study of God's words, or freedom of all external concerns. Others say that contemplation is freedom to see through the spectacles of wisdom, to a very high magnification indeed. Others say that it is a kind of treatise on wise looking at the soul, spread out as it were to see greatness. Others say rightly that contemplation is joy in heavenly things. Others say, with even greater justice, that it is the death of physical desires achieved by raising up the joys of the mind.

I think that contemplation means having in one's mind the joyful song of God's love and all the sweet praise of angels. We call this 'jubilation', which is the goal of the prayer of perfection and of devotion in this life. That is the possession of the truly happy mind which sees with spiritual eyes the Everlasting Lover and calls out with a loud voice in praise of him. It is the ultimate and really perfect form of death to this life. The psalm on the subject says: Blessed the man who rejoices in contemplating God. No one who is apart from God can rejoice in Jesus or taste the sweetness of his love unless he or she always desires to burn with the fire of everlasting love. Patiently and humbly, that person must be made beautiful by cleansing of mind and body, to be adorned with spiritual jewels and raised up into contemplation, and unceasingly seek for healing virtues – which cleanse us from our wretched sins in this life and free us from all pain in the blessed endless life hereafter.

Even while exiled in this world you will be made worthy to feel the wonderful joy of God's love.

So don't be slow to check yourself by prayer and examination of conscience. Don't neglect spiritual meditation, for such spiritual works, and weeping and sorrow within, will surely kindle the fire of Christ's love in you, and all the virtues and gifts of the Holy Spirit will be poured into your heart. Begin with the practice of voluntary poverty, so that all you want in this world is to live soberly, chastely and humbly before God and mankind. Sometimes poverty causes us to have nothing, but it is a great virtue to wish to have nothing.

Of course we have many desires. Even the most perfect accept necessities, for no one would be perfect who refused to take the very basics that are necessary to staying alive.

The perfect man or woman must live thus: forsaking and despising everything for God's sake, and yet eating and wearing all that is necessary. If he or she has any want at any time, then there must be no complaint; love of God is the answer, and to refuse superfluity as far as possible.

The warmer anyone grows in the heat of everlasting light, the humbler in all hardship. Anyone who is truly meek despises himself or herself and is not provoked to anger. If we give ourselves up to meditation we can rise up to behold heavenly things by the acuity of our purified mind's eye; then, even if we fall ill, we shall be filled with heavenly joy. Then we do not stride out proudly, looking for external things, but rejoice only (but marvellously) in the sweetness of God's love, so wonderfully full of joy that we might well have been ravished in a dream!

That is the nature of contemplation, and, if we practise spiritual works long and assiduously, we shall reach the point where we contemplate everlasting things. The mind is so held that it sees shadows of heavenly things as in a glass, for while we live by faith we see only as shadows, as if in a mirror. If our spiritual eye is open to that spiritual light, it may not see the light as it actually is, yet feel nevertheless *that* it *is*, and cleave to it with undreamed-of joy and heat. Hence the psalm says: As its darkness, so its light.

Even though all the darkness of sin is departed from a holy soul, and the mind is purified and enlightened, while it is mortal it may not perceive perfect joy. Of course holy and contemplative men look on God with a clear vision (for their minds are opened and all barriers between God and them are thrown down); their hearts are purified and they see the inhabitants of heaven. Christ also gives us his consoling darkness and speaks to us in a pillar of cloud, but what we feel is truly joyful.

It is truly perfect love when anyone still mortal rejoices only in God, and wants nothing and desires nothing except God and for God's sake. And so we know that holiness does not consist in the crying out of the heart, or in tears, or in external works, but in the sweetness of perfect love and heavenly contemplation. Many people melt with tears yet suddenly turn to evil, but no one will concern himself or herself with worldly things after truly tasting Everlasting Love.

Weeping and sorrow are proper to the unconverted and to beginners. Rejoicing in contemplation, however, is proper to the perfect alone. If we do penance for a long time, even though our conscience pricks us we surely feel that we have not as yet attained to perfect penance. Then our 'tears are bread to us day and night', for as long as we punish ourselves with sighs and tears we have not reached the sweetness of contemplation.

We have to work very hard indeed to get contemplative sweetness, but when we do get it the joy is unbelievable. Of course it is not something that we can win by our own merit, but God's gift, and never yet, from the beginning of the world to this very day, has anyone ever been ravished in the contemplation of Everlasting Love without completely giving up all the vanities of this world.

What is more, we have to be experienced in sound, devout prayer, before contemplating heavenly joys.

Contemplation is a very pleasurable and desirable practice. It makes us glad and does us no harm. It makes us joyful, and we feel tiredness only when it departs from us.

Anyone who is inflamed by the fire of the Holy Spirit needs great rest of mind and body.

Yet many people are unable to rest in mind because of all their pointless thoughts. They can't do as the psalmist says: Rid yourself of worldly vanities and see that I am God.

These wandering hearts cannot taste and see how sweet our Lord is, they cannot savour the sweetness of the heights of contemplation. Every contemplative loves solitude, which is needed if the contemplative is not to be parted from his or her fervent desires.

A very contemplative person is often thought to be a fool, for his or her mind is so intent on unseen things, and so inflamed by the love of Christ, that the very stance of the body changes. The contemplative seems to stand apart from all other human beings as a child of God, and to other people seems raving mad.

While the soul gathers everything within itself in unending joy of love, it does not flow outwards to physical things. Because it feeds on inward affections, it is hardly astonishing that it should sigh and say: 'Who will give me you, my Brother, so that I can find you and kiss you?'

A devout soul which practises contemplation and is filled with everlasting love despises the vanities of this world, and wants only to enjoy Jesus and to be in the splendid company of the angels, undisturbed by worldly changes and troubles.

There is nothing better and more joyful than the grace of contemplation, which lifts us out of the habits and practices of this world, and brings us to God. The grace of contemplation is nothing other than the being of joy. And what is perfect joy but grace confirmed in us, so that we stay joyful and happy in glorious eternity, living with saints and angels in endless joy? Above all it means knowing God truly, and loving him perfectly. It means seeing his Majesty shining, and in all eternity loving with wonderful joy and melody him to whom be worship and joy with thanksgiving in the world of worlds. Amen.